Santa Claus:

Is He For Your Child?

John L. Hoh, Jr.

ISBN 978-0-6151-85774

HoneyMilk Publications
7253 N. 86th. St., 201
Milwaukee WI 53224

Honey Milk
Publications
Fine publications of a spiritual nature

CHAPTER ONE

When I was growing up, the onslaught didn't begin until Thanksgiving Day when the Christmas sales began running during the football games. Today the jolly old elf can't wait—sometimes he's out with the Halloween displays or even hawking "Christmas in July." In the minds of many Santa Claus, with his red suit and white beard, is equated with Christmas. Even people that abhor anything religious honor this particular patron saint every Christmas!

It is sad that more people think about Santa than about our Lord Jesus Christ at Christmastime. For the two today stand directly opposed to each other. Jesus offers full and free forgiveness of all of our sins through his innocent blood shed on the cross of Calvary. Santa offers toys and goodies to those who are "good little boys and girls." That we have two diametrically opposing themes at Christmas is bad enough; that the diabolical legalism of Santa Claus is gaining more acceptance and popularity is a tragedy.

The myth of Santa has grown to gigantic proportions. He is able to know all, to judge each and every child, to make reindeer fly and do all these things at the North Pole!

Obviously Santa has slowly taken the place of God, doing things which only God can do.

Unfortunately, this "god" is a legalistic "god", dispensing gifts only upon those who deserve them. As a popular Christmas song states:

> *He knows when you are sleeping,*
> *He knows when you're awake,*
> *He knows if you've been bad or good,*
> *So be good for goodness sake!*
> *So you better not pout, you better not cry*
> *You better watch out, I'm telling you why--*
> *Santa Claus is coming to town!*

Many of us are familiar with Rudolph, the Red-nose Reindeer. Again, another tale that reveals that this "saint" is less than saintly. Rudolph is shunted aside—until he proves his worth "one foggy Christmas Eve." A far cry from the God-man Jesus Christ who preached repentance and forgiveness to all sinners in the New Testament!

This treatise looks at the origins of Santa Claus. It looks at how the myth started, how it grew, where the various names that St. Nick is also known by originated and how we got our jolly old elf that many today have come to know and love.

The main point of this treatise is to point out how the myth of Santa Claus is diametrically opposed to the truth of Jesus Christ. Whether we use our Christian freedom to pay some honor to St. Nicholas or Santa Claus in our home or not is for each Christian to decide for himself or herself. But as in any decision we make, the best decision is an informed decision. This treatise sets out to give you that information in order to make an intelligent decision.

Foremost is that to God alone be the Glory, Forever and ever, Amen.

CHAPTER TWO
Origins: The Man Behind the Myth

The lineage of Santa Claus is almost always traced back to a bishop in the village of Myra, Nicholas by name. As with many famous people in the early church, legends grew up surrounding miraculous or charitable deeds allegedly done by this saintly bishop. As the years go by, the legends evolved so that the original story has little semblance to the later versions.

When we compare many of the saintly legends to the miracles recorded in the Bible some startling differences pop out. The Bible records Jesus' miracles with a high degree of similitude when the Synoptic Gospels (Matthew, Mark, and Luke) record these miracles. However, the saintly legends do not maintain the same degree of integrity. An example is the tale of the three virgins, the original tale of St. Nicholas' exploits. Some of the legends record that the gold for each daughter was secretly tossed into the window (or some say placed at the door) on three successive nights; some have a span of several years, as each daughter comes of a marriageable age. Some say that the father was a peasant; others insist that he was a

7

businessman down on his luck (though he was either a poor businessman or didn't know how to save up for his daughters' weddings—St. Nicholas had to bail him out three times!).

What we actually do know about Nicholas, I'm afraid, wouldn't even cover a sheet of paper. Like Shakespeare, Nicholas of Myra is an enigma of history. So little is known, in fact, that the Roman Church in 1969 questioned whether or not the bishop/saint actually existed (Giblin: *The Truth About Santa Claus*, p. 5). The earliest stories come from three sources that date no earlier than 500 AD: *Vita Per Metaphrasten* (*Life According to Metaphrastes*, written by a Simeon Metaphrastes), *Vita Per Michaelem* (*Life According to Michael*) and *Vita Compilata* (*The Life Compiled*). Of the three, the *Vita Compilata* is the most comprehensive and is the only source of the names of Nicholas' parents (Epiphanus and Nonna) (Ebon: *Saint Nicholas: Life and Legend*, p. 4).

The bishop lived in the fourth century of our Lord. Biographers have written that his family "was not so rich as to be boastful, but they had enough to support themselves and still give to the poor" (Giblin: *The Truth About Santa Claus*, p. 6). The *Vita Compilata* reports about the family:

> They were naturally pious people who did not have to go
> in for such dramatic proof of their faith as walking
> barefoot on hot tar or holding it in their hands. (Ebon:
> *Saint Nicholas: Life and Legend*, p. 9)

It appears that Nicholas' mother was sterile and prayed in the manner of Hannah (1 Samuel 1:11; 2:26) (Ebon: *Saint Nicholas: Life and Legend*, p. 9). When Nicholas was 12 or 13 his parents died from a plague that hit Patara. Nicholas, left an orphan, was raised by his uncle, a bishop living in a nearby community (Giblin: *The Truth About Santa Claus*, p. 6).

Nicholas was born in Patara, possibly in 280 AD. Patara is just down the coast from Myra, where Nicholas would later serve as bishop (Ebon: *Saint Nicholas: Life and Legend*, p. 9). These towns, incidently, were visited by the Apostle Paul himself. Luke records that Paul set sail for Palestine from Patara at the conclusion of his third missionary journey (Acts 21:1) and stopped at Myra on his way to Rome (Acts 27:5).

Today these cities are part of the country of Turkey and under Moslem control. When the Turks conquered Myra, Nicholas' bones were transferred for safekeeping—which adds a delightful tale I will relate later!

Many of the tales talk of an infant Nicholas abstaining from his mother's breast on fast days (Wednesdays and Fridays) until after sundown. He also **prematurely** stood in his wash basin and crib (emphasis mine). Metaphrastes reports:
> [Nicholas] showed from the beginning he wanted to
> please God. He appeared to be a good student, who
> attended church regularly, helping with the older men so
> as to benefit from their example and guidance (Ebon:
> Saint Nicholas: Life and Legend, p. 9).

Nicholas had an uncle, also named Nicholas, who was a bishop in a neighboring community. It seems some of the legends that were originally attributed to the uncle soon were ascribed to the nephew. The uncle had his nephew help with church services.

It was here that young Nick learned the text of prayers while showing a remarkably quick mind and sincere devotion. Nicholas was ordained into the priesthood at the age of 19.

Metaphrastes writes that at the ordination the uncle delivered the address. In this address Nicholas' uncle "prophesied" that his nephew would offer guidance and consolation to many, would himself attain the rank of bishop and "live a life of enlightenment." Simeon Metaphrastes goes on to report:
> From the minute the saint became a priest, one can
> hardly keep count of the virtue and goodness he spread

> *about him, of the nights spent at his devotions, days of*
> *fasting, steadfast goodwill, and his prayers for all.*
> *Observing this, his uncle, the Bishop Nicholas, found the*
> *young man's*
> *eagerness admirable. And when he went on a pilgrimage*
> *to Jerusalem, the Bishop left Nicholas as his deputy, to*
> *oversee the monastery he had built, and which he had*
> *called New Zion. The saint administered both the*
> *Bishopric and the Monastery as competently as if he had*
> *been the bishop himself* (Ebon: *Saint Nicholas: Life and*
> *Legend*, p. 10).

> *NOTE: Notice that Simeon Metaphrastes refers to*
> *Nicholas as "saint," thus betraying that his work*
> *came into existence long after Nicholas died!*

The only mention of the bishop's life and work are bound in myths.
One such story deals with his consecration as bishop:

> After his return from Palestine Nicholas dwelt in the
> city of Myra, where he lived unknown in great humility.
> At length the bishop of Myra died, and a revelation was
> made to the clergy to the effect that the first man who
> should come to church the next morning was the man
> whom God had chosen for their bishop. So when
> Nicholas came early to church to pray, as was his
> custom, the clergy led him into the church and
> consecrated him bishop (M'Clintock & Strong:
> *Cyclopaedia of Biblical, Theological, and Ecclesiastical*
> *Literature [VII--New-Pes]*, 61)

He does appear on the roster attending the council of Nicea, which
was called to deal with the Arian controversy. The controversy dealt
with Arius' denial of the deity of Christ. Nicholas is on record as
upholding the doctrine of Christ's divinity.

A legend goes on to state that, while Arius was speaking, Nicholas
became so enraged that he walked up to Arius and slapped him. As it

was unlawful to slap someone in the presence of the emperor, the bishops concluded that Nicholas must be stripped of his bishop's garments and placed under arrest. It was while Nicholas was imprisoned that evening that Jesus appeared and asked Nicholas why he was imprisoned. Nicholas replied that it was because of his love for the Lord. Jesus then frees him and gives him a volume of Scripture while the Holy Mother returns his bishop's garments to him. The jailor found Nicholas unshackled and reading the Bible the next morning. When the emperor heard of these events, he begs forgiveness. Whether we can take stock in any part of the legend is dubious. But it is the attendance records of the First Council of Nicea that form the main proof for the historical existence of Nicholas, bishop of Myra (Ebon: *Saint Nicholas: Life and Legend*, pp. 34-35)

It does seem quite possible that Nicholas suffered under the reign of Diocletian. Stories abound of his imprisonment for over five years under Diocletian. He was then released when Constantine came to power. No doubt the presence of two regimes back to back, one religiously persecuting the Church, the other recognizing it as a legal religion, shows the numbers and the political power of Christians. One emperor no doubt saw the Christian religion as a threat; the other employing it as a political ally. As one of the leaders (as an ordained priest) Nicholas would not only not be spared persecution, but be one of the first persecuted. It is interesting that we have no "miraculous events" of the Nicholas/Santa Claus legend recorded for us from his imprisonment. He was granted a bishopric after his release and his legends seem to begin with that promotion (although some sources record the legend of the three virgins occurring before even his ordination. More on this later).

On 6 December 343 AD, Nicholas, Bishop of Myra, died. (Note: The early Church celebrated the date of a believer's death, since this was their "birthday into eternal life." To celebrate one's actual birth date was considered pagan.) Stories of his deeds were already common at the time of his death. By 450 AD churches in Greece and Asia Minor were named in his honor. In 800 AD Nicholas was canonized as a saint in the Eastern Catholic Church (Giblin: *The Truth About Santa Claus*, pp. 8-10). No mention seems to be made of when or if the Western Church recognized his canonization.

However, in 1970, the Vatican calender listed December 6 as the "Second Sunday of Advent" rather than "Feast of St. Nicholas." The uproar that this caused showed that the cult of St. Nicholas is alive and well (Ebon: *Saint Nicholas: Life and Legend*, p. 79). The aftermath of this sequence of events will also be looked at later.

In conclusion about the bare facts of Nicholas' life, we have this footnote from Will Durant:

> St. Nicholas, in the fourth century, modestly filled the Episcopal see of Myra in Lycia, never dreaming that he was to be the patron saint of Russia, of thieves and boys and girls, and at last, in his Dutch name as Santa Claus, to enter into the Christmas mythology of half the Christian world. (Durant: *The Story of Civilization [4--The Age of Faith]*, p. 62.

CHAPTER THREE
The Legends of the Three Virgins

This treatise first looks at the various legends that have attached themselves to the cult of St. Nicholas. We see how they have evolved to contribute to the Santa Claus of today. It also takes a critical look at these legends to point out how they oppose the clear teachings of Scripture and serve to undermine the faith of Christians throughout the ages.

The first legend that we look at is probably the most popular legend: The Legend of the Three Virgins. What the legends throughout the ages have agreed upon are these points: A man has three daughters but cannot afford to support them or provide a dowry.

Slavery or prostitution is considered so that the burden is lifted off of the father. In the end, St. Nicholas comes through and provides the aid necessary for the daughters' salvation. Of course, the kindly saint does this under cover of darkness, but the father awaits in the shadows for the third visit to learn the identity of his benefactor. These are the points that the legends all contain. As I said before, there are major differences in the various legends that we have available to us.

When this alleged incident took place even the various stories do not agree. Robin Crichton, in his book *Who is Santa Claus? The True Story Behind A Living Legend*, reports that his sources report its occurrence "before Nicholas enters the monastery" (Crichton: *Who is Santa Claus? The True Story Behind A Living Legend*, p. 19). Yet Giblin's sources relate that "the father hid in the shadows and spied the kindly bishop" (Giblin: *The Truth About Santa Claus*, p. 17)— obviously much later than the time that Crichton reports! Ebon reports that this happened before he became a priest, placing the event obviously before Giblin's account, but closer to Crichton's (Ebon: *St. Nicholas: Life and Legend*, p. 10). We thus see that the legend grew and evolved with each generation making its own changes.

That there were three daughters is agreed upon. When these daughters all received their "Visit from St. Nicholas" is again a matter of conjecture. Crichton records that the visits were in three successive nights (*Who is Santa Claus? The True Story Behind A Living Legend*, p. 20). Yet many other legends report several years between the first visit and the last visit (Ebon: *Saint Nicholas: Life and Legend*, p. 11).

Just who was the father and what was his occupation? The *Cyclopedia of Biblical, Theological, and Ecclesiastical Literature* refers to the father as a poor nobleman (*Vol. VII*, p. 62). Ebon says that he was a "down-on-his-luck merchant" (*Saint Nicholas: Life and Legend*, p. 10). There is no way of knowing precisely who the recipient of Nick's goodwill is even if the story were true.

Questions also arise as to how the luck-less family would extricate itself out of its quandary. Obviously there was little money for the daughters to be honorably married. But who made the decision that the eldest (or even all three daughters) should be sold? And was it a sale into slavery or prostitution? Crichton records:

Also that the eldest, after the daughters had talked the problem over, would willingly enter the brothel "to abandon (herself) to the synne of lecherye so that by the gayne and wynning of (her) infamye (the others might) be sustained" (Who is Santa Claus? The True Story Behind A Living Legend, p. 19).

Ebon writes that the father had made the decision to sell his eldest daughter into slavery or prostitution when Nick intervened. As if this wasn't unscrupulous enough, he planned on doing the same to the other daughters, forcing Nick to intervene each time before being caught the third time! (Ebon: *Saint Nicholas: Life and Legend*, pp. 10-11)

In every recording of this tale, St. Nicholas gives a gift of money for the girls' dowries. We may today question whether this was a practical and wise gift considering that the father obviously had some problems handling money! How the money comes into the house differs. In some Nick tosses the bags of gold coins through an open window. Another version has Nick tossing the bags through smoke holes in the wall and into stockings that the sisters had hung up to dry (was Santa a good shot, all-knowing, or just lucky in his tosses?).

Regardless of whether or not any of these events actually happened, we can see that any grain of truth is lost among layers of myth and legend. No doubt twists are given by each culture and/or generation to reinforce certain beliefs of that time or region. Where Scripture is consistent in its narrative, the Saint Nicholas legends all reflect cultural biases. And there are hidden dangers and snares in these stories.

One needs to question the actions of the family. Was it necessary to sell the daughter(s) into slavery or, worse, prostitution? Even if this occurred before Nicholas entered the monastery, wasn't he righteous enough, according to legend, to know the difference between right and wrong? (Cf. Chapter Two). Especially as a bishop Nicholas should have known right from wrong. A good bishop of Christ ought to use the Law, first of all to show that the actions about to be taken are contrary to the holy will of God.

Nowhere is there any mention that Nicholas also offered the Gospel hope and comfort. Instead he is seen as a good church worker who has a big heart and generous purse to help those thinking about the most drastic, and ungodly, of measures. Nowhere is there found that the father understood grace, forgiveness or repentance. What happens after the tale we never know—the kindly saint gets his credit. The act becomes the source for artwork in the church (further reinforcing the myth) and is carried on in Christmas/St. Nick traditions all over the world (to be related later).

Had Saint Nicholas been as "righteous" as the legends claim, why didn't he then use the opportunity of bailing the father out as a vivid illustration of our salvation? For totally by grace Christ bought us from sin, death and the devil. Yet Luther reminds us:

*"[Jesus] has redeemed me, a lost and condemned creature, purchased and won me from all sins, from death, and from the power of the devil, **not with gold or silver, but with His holy, precious blood and with His innocent sufferings and death**; That I should be His own, and live under Him in His kingdom, and serve Him in everlasting righteousness, innocence, and blessedness; even as He is risen from death, lives and reigns to all eternity.*

This is most certainly true.

(Bold emphasis mine) (Gausewitz, ed., *Doctor Martin Luther's Small Catechism*, p. 5)

St. Peter reminds us "knowing that you were not redeemed with corruptible things, like silver or gold, from your aimless conduct received by tradition of your fathers, but with the precious blood of Christ, as a lamb without blemish and without spot" (1 Peter 1:18-

19). In Acts 3 we see Peter and John confronted with a lame man who also needs help. Here Peter says to the man "Silver and gold I do not have, but what I do have I will give you: In the name of Jesus Christ of Nazareth, rise up and walk" (Acts 3:1-10). Yet Nick's gift is the "corruptible gold" and the Gospel treasure is not shared.

The legends also have the kindly saint (or bishop) sneaking around at night under cover of darkness. The result is not that God receives the glory, but that St. Nicholas is praised for this "good deed." Simeon Metaphrastes opines:

> Now that we know of this one deed, we are able to understand the other achievements he tried to keep secret, seeking to avoid the praise of men and hoping only for God's approval. Yet, the more he tried to hide his qualities, the more did God reveal his true nature, in order to honor him, just as he had honored God through his deeds of mercy.
> (Bold emphasis mine)
> (Ebon: *Saint Nicholas: Life and Legend*, p. 11)

No where in the Scriptures do the men of God do their deeds under cover of darkness. They act in public and publicly give the honor and glory to God! In some cases the deed lands the messenger of God into prison (Acts 16: 16-24). Sometimes others not related to the miracle try to cash in (2 Kings 5:20-27). But always the deed is done in public and publicly the glory is given to God. Only once has anything good in Scripture been done in darkness. That one time is when Nicodemus comes to Jesus at night to learn about the kingdom of God. From this meeting we have that sweet Gospel message of John 3:16!

In one legend Nicholas swears the father to strict silence when caught. The father promises—only to reveal all on his death bed! Whenever I hear of deathbed confessions, however, they are usually in the context of someone who knows that the end is near and seeks to clear his soul before meeting his maker! Does this particular father, then, feel guilty about the whole series of events?

The doctrine of Saint Nicholas appears to be a doctrine of work righteousness. Like the Pharisees and teachers of the Law in Jesus day, he does these good works "for God's approval." He apparently loses sight of (or the legends blatantly leave out) the fact that any approval that we may gain from God is solely through the blood of Christ.

That this approval also is not shared with and encouraged in the family is a second blight on the reputation of St. Nicholas. We can also see elements of a social gospel in this particular legend. The "Church" antes up to prevent a social evil from taking place. No doubt the people embraced these stories with the hope that later clergy would open the purse to cure social ills (such as poverty).

That the legend would be popular at Christmas time is dangerous. It takes attention away from the grand and glorious gift of God the Father to all mankind. God sent his Son to free us from our slavery to sin, death and the Devil; purchasing us with the innocent, pure and incorruptible blood of the Lamb and comforting us with the Word and Sacrament, the means of grace through which the Holy Spirit has chosen to work!

CHAPTER FOUR
The Saint Becomes the Patron of Sailors

Very early in the vast legend and lore of St. Nicholas are the stories regarding Nicholas' providence for sailors. That sailors the world over would have a patron saint shouldn't be startling. Within a century after Christianity became legal in the Roman Empire the "patron saints" took over the duties formerly held by the gods of Greek and Roman mythology. Yet with Nicholas we see an almost universal acceptance by sailors of this bishop for their patron. What are the tales that are used to cement this belief?

There are many tales with many variations but usually playing on the same theme: Nicholas bails out sailors caught in storms and/or shipwrecks.

It is in the East that Nicholas enjoys his fame as the patron saint of sailors. Indeed he is the patron saint of the sailors in Western nations also, but that is usually eclipsed by his reputation as patron of children. The Dutch for one have many St. Nicholas customs devoted to their shipping industry!

There are tales that allegedly take place before Nicholas' ascension to the office of bishop. Interestingly, some of these tales do not put the sailors in a good light (of course, neither does the father appear virtuous in the previous tale mentioned!). Some of the tales relate the spirit of the dead bishop appearing and either warning the crew of a coming storm or rescuing the crew from the storm.

One tale relates that Nicholas was sleeping and dreamed of a fierce storm endangering the boat. He warned the crew, assuring them that it would pass. However the storm does come up and a member of the crew fell from a mast to his death. When the storm subsides, Nicholas brings the young man back to life (Ebon: *Saint Nicholas: Life and Legend*, p. 1).

This legend seems to give birth to even more legends. Allegedly this occurred while Nicholas was sailing to the Holy Land (pre-bishopric pilgrimage). When the boat arrives, many sick came to him and were healed. Nicholas had planned to stay several weeks, but "an angel of the Lord ordered him" to return home immediately. He was promised by the ship's crew to be taken directly to Patara, but was actually deceived because the crew wanted to go home first (no mention of where "home" was). Divine intervention brought a storm that broke the rudders and led the boat to Patara. The frightened sailors, naturally, beg for forgiveness. Nicholas responds: "From now on, don't try to fool anyone" (Ebon: *Saint Nicholas: Life and Legend*, p. 13). Imagine making someone your patron saint who wouldn't allow fellow tradesmen to see home!

Another legend has the saint appear to a captain in a dream. Handing him three gold coins, he asks him to sail into Myra. The captain thought it was only a dream—until he realized that he was holding the three coins. Naturally the captain changes course (Ebon: *Saint Nicholas: Life and Legend*, pp. 41-42). How money propels people to do things they don't plan on doing. Yet I don't recall the angel paying Joseph to abandon his plan to desert Mary or to take his family into Egypt. The wise men weren't bribed to avoid Herod and return home by a different route.

The degree to which St. Nicholas is cast as the patron saint of sailors is found in the exploration of the New World. The Vikings dedicated a cathedral in Greenland to the saint. Columbus named a port after St. Nicholas when he landed in Haiti on his first voyage. The original name of Jacksonville, Florida, was St. Nicholas Ferry (Ebon: *Saint Nicholas: Life and Legend*, p. 87). The original ship that brought Dutch immigrants to New Amsterdam (today New York) was named the *Goede Vrowe* (*Good Woman*). The figure on the prow was not a woman, however, but an icon of St. Nicholas (Jones: *The Santa Claus Book*, p. 23). No doubt many sailors in their time of need called out and invoked the name of Saint Nicholas in the fashion that Luther cried out: "St. Anne help me! I will become a monk." (Saint Anne is allegedly the mother of Mary within which legends also abound that relate Mary's birth as having identical circumstances of Samuel's and Nicholas' birth. Anne was also the patron saint of miners, the occupation of Luther's father.)

The *Dictionary of Christian Lore and Legend* (Metford, p. 181) comments on Nicholas' popularity with sailors:

> *One of Nicholas' attributes is an anchor, because he was adopted as the patron saint of sailors when he answered the prayers of some mariners lost in a storm, joining them in their sinking ship and bringing them safely to land. Many harbour (sic) churches are therefore dedicated to him. His association with the sea is commemorated annually at Bari, Italy, where part of his relics were transferred from Myra in 1087. His image is taken out in a boat on his feast day and brought back to his church at night, escorted by a torchlight procession.*

Many of the nautical tales of Nicholas have a secondary theme of famine. The intervention by Nicholas often was necessitated by a famine in Asia Minor. Nicholas (or his apparition) would convince a ship's captain to stop and deliver grain at a famine-ravaged port. Of course Nicholas promises that the captain would still arrive at his destination with the full load, much as Elijah promised the widow of Zarephath oil and flour that would never run out (1 Kings 17:8-16). This variety of the ancient mariner tales obviously does not put the sailors themselves in a good light. They come off looking greedy and oblivious to the suffering in nearby ports. In some cases, as seen before, the captain or crew is bribed in order to carry out these missions of mercy.

Why sailors have adopted Nicholas as their patron saint and not Paul is amazing.

Luke records for us in Acts 27 about Paul's boat trip. Paul warns the crew about an impending storm, only to be ignored. Paul prays on behalf of the sailors. He publicly acknowledges who his God is and what he would do (spare their lives when the boat is wrecked). The cargo of wheat was discarded for survival without a promise from Paul that it would be restored.

When the sailors attempt to kill all the prisoners to keep them from escaping (allowing a prisoner to escape was a capital offense in Roman law), it wasn't Paul who spared his own life, but God moved the captain to restrain the sailors from carrying out their plan. Upon arriving at Malta, where the shipwreck occurred, Paul conducted the ministry of the Lord while he was there.

Of course the account of Paul's sea journey, shipwreck and survival are not adorned with the tapestry of supernatural deeds as the tales that concern St. Nicholas. Nevertheless we see that Paul is working for the Lord. The myths of Nicholas paint him as a self-serving and self-promoting saint.

Indeed the truth of the Gospel does not appear in these tales. Nicholas does not ask the sailors to help relieve famine by reminding them of God's blessings they have received. Nicholas also resorts to opening his own purse to cure the problem.

22

Contrast this with how Paul deals with fellow Christians in helping to relieve the famine in Jerusalem (Acts 11:27-30; Romans 15:24-32; 1 Corinthians 16:1-4; 2 Corinthians 8:1-9:15; Philippians 4:10-20).

Contrast Paul's words and actions and motivations with Nicholas' words, actions and motivations. The spirit of the two men is definitely different. Paul's motivation is the Gospel; Nicholas of myth is motivated and motivates by the Law. Nicholas' insignia might be an anchor, but it is Paul who presents the true anchor of our lives and faith—the Gospel message of full and free forgiveness in the blood of the crucified Lamb of God and sealed for us in his resurrection. And as was pointed out in the previous chapter, the myth points out a cleric who is generous with the purse to solve societal problems.

CHAPTER FIVE

The Innkeeper's Choice Cuts:
Were They From Seminary Students or
Children?

Another tale, or family of tales, helps to launch St. Nicholas as the patron saint of seminary students. These tales would change over the years as St. Nicholas also became the patron saint of children. Earlier versions of these tales have as victims seminary students who stopped for the night at the wrong inn. Later versions would have small children as the victims, although no mention is made of whether the parents of the children were present or why these children would be alone.

The tale basically finds Nicholas on his way to Nicea during a famine. When Nicholas stops at an inn, he wonders how the innkeeper is able to serve him pot roast. Of course it couldn't possibly be that maybe the innkeeper couldn't afford to buy grain during a famine and thus he butchered his cow(s) for meat (much as the modern American farmer does). Instead the bishop catches the innkeeper in the process of butchering and preparing to chop up three little boys. These three boys are then brought back to life. However, no mention is made of the "victim" of whom Nicholas must have allegedly ate (Crichton: *Who is Santa Claus? The True Story Behind a Living Legend*, p. 25; Metford: *Dictionary of Christian Lore and Legend*, p. 181).

Again the innkeeper is chastised for his crimes. He is not arrested for trial, at least not that any legends mention. If the innkeeper were repentant, he does not receive the Gospel comfort, but a stern warning from the Law. Also, the tale evolves with the passage of time. Legends differ on the victims being theology students, college students or small children. The legend made him the patron saint of endangered travelers, but was later modified as the saint more and more patronized children.

One wonders, then, since Nicholas seemingly befriended students and travelers, why Luther didn't cry out to Nicholas instead of St. Anne!

Correcting injustices done to innocents was another theme that wraps around the Nicholas legends. One famous work that advanced this view is a document written during the reign of Justinian, the *Praxis de Stratilatis* (*The Practice of the Generals*).

This work dealt with three generals, named Ursos, Nepotianos and Herpylion. The book contained three parts or stories, each one portraying Nicholas as the righter of wrongs (Ebon: *Saint Nicholas: Life and Legend*, p. 20)

The first tale deals with the three generals when they are sent by Constantine to put down the Phrygian revolts. Because of storms, they are forced to stop en route at Myra. The soldier-sailors go into town, soldier-sailors are wont to do with time on their hands. Although they went for provisions, they soon get into fights with the local populace. Nicholas has to hunt down the generals, who are unaware that the fighting is taking place. After the generals subdue their soldiers, military and civilians join together to repair the damage. After Nicholas fed the three generals (no mention is made whether the soldiers were also fed), he sends them on their way (Ebon: *Saint Nicholas: Life and Legend*, p. 21).

The second part of the *Praxis* deals with the imminent beheading of three innocent men by a corrupt man by the name of Eustathios. Nicholas, with the aid of the three generals, rushes to the execution site. There the sword is seized from the hands of the executioner. Eustathios rushes to the town square to see what was delaying the execution. Confronted by the bishop and the three generals, Eustathios confesses the injustice that was performed. He is forgiven and the two parties part in "mutual charity" (Ebon: *Saint Nicholas: Life and Legend*, p. 22).

The third part relates the following tale. The generals are successful in putting down the revolt. However, rivals are jealous of the generals' successes and create lies concerning the three generals. An official is then bribed first to imprison, then to kill the three generals. The bribe-taker, Evlavios by name, fears to have the blood of the generals on his hands, so tells Constantine lies about the generals. Since Constantine was a man of quick decisions, he immediately condemned the three generals to death.

The three generals turn to their good friend, Nicholas of Myra, in prayer. Nicholas then comes to Constantine and Evlavios in dreams. He threatens Constantine with the loss of his life in a war unless he frees the three generals. He tells Evlavios that he shouldn't take bribes and to right the wrong. Constantine frees the generals, telling them to become monks, and sends gifts to Nicholas. It is in the *Praxis*, however, that we find any mention of Nicholas ever deferring thanks and praise to God (Ebon: *Saint Nicholas: Life and Legend*, pp. 23-26).

Another strain of myths is introduced by this work. Through this strain Nicholas is now also the patron of those falsely accused and rescues the condemned innocents on the eve of their executions (nothing like being melodramatic!).

An extension of Nicholas' role as protector of children is a logical extension. In order to retain a clientele, children need to be born. For these children to be born legitimately, maidens need to be wed. Dr. Adrian de Groot, a professor of psychology at the University of Amsterdam, writes the following:

> *In the Middle Ages, St. Nicholas was not only the protector of children but also the patron of parenthood, the fosterer of family fertility. He must have been invoked many, many times by married couples who wanted children* (Ebon: *Saint Nicholas: Life and Legend*, p. 53).

French maidens were particularly desirous of the saint's intercession to find them a husband. Many aspects of French Nicholalotry were characteristic of long-forgotten, possibly pagan, rituals with sexually symbolic overtones. One example occurred at Chapelle St.-Nicholas-des-Bois-aux-Bìards as young, marriage-minded women would climb a rock outcropping. Other young maidens climbed a monolith at Notre Dame de Déliverance and placed a coin into the monolith for hope. Maidens visiting Fécamp Seine-Intérieure used to throw pebbles at a statue of St. Nicholas (reminiscent of one throwing pebbles at the window of a true love). Strong in Normandy, but also found in other French provinces, virgins would recite in the manner of schoolchildren: "*Patron des filles, Saint Nicholas: mariez-nous, ne tardez pas,*" meaning "Saint Nicholas, patron of girls: get me married without delay." Another jingle echoed the sentiment: "*Saint Nicholas, marie les filles avec les garcons*" ("Saint Nicholas, marry the girls to the boys"). Soon the duties of the patron of happy marriages was broadened to include providing happiness and wealth. December 6 was then considered a lucky day and was desired for the completion of important business transactions, purchases and marriages (Ebon: *Saint Nicholas: Life and Legend*, p. 54).

As we see the evolution of the fame and legend of the saint, the progression is predictable and constant. The fact that wealth came to be considered a domain of Nicholas manifests itself. Pawn brokers adopt Nicholas as their patron, so that today the symbol of pawn-brokers is the three golden balls that comprise Nicholas' saintly symbol.

The legend that starts this strain of the myth arise from a Jewish lender who lent money to a Christian borrower. The Christian takes an oath in Nicholas' name. When Nicholas defends his honor by making the Christian repay his debt, he then takes on the duties as protector and guarantor of solemn oaths. Knights and crusaders then prepare for combat by taking oaths in the name of Nicholas. In Holland the phrase "I swear by Nicholas the Saint..." became commonplace, much like the American "By George." How deeply did Nicholas become imbedded in the field of trade and commerce? Those same three golden balls that are the symbol of the saint and the trademark of his patrons, the pawnbrokers, also became a part of the coat of arms of the Medici family, a family that dominated the European trading and banking fields! (Ebon: *Saint Nicholas: Life and Legend*, p. 69)

We see in the cult of Nicholas an attempt to adopt the saint as a spokesman and defender of the teachings, ideas, and beliefs of each particular group. During the American Civil War, President Abraham Lincoln was once asked if he thought God was on the side of the North. Lincoln remarked that it wasn't important that God be on the side of the North, but that the North be on the side of God! How often don't people in the church seek God to be on their side, not realizing that the important thing is to be found on God's side. Many seek to validate their message and agenda through the blessing of God and/or saints, not to submit to the will and message of God.

The coming sections look at the adoration of saints in the Church. As we view this brief history, then the beliefs of Saint Nicholas in the various nations, the fact leaps out that mankind does indeed seek the advancement of its own causes through the church structure and its attendant beliefs and institutions. Foremost, in advancing human causes and ideas, the true message of the Gospel is lost. Our sinfulness is placed in stark contrast to the alleged holiness of the saints. Our meager attempts to atone for our sins do not find solace in these tales. The true message of full and free forgiveness is absent and lost in the myths of the saints. Nowhere is this more true than in the myths and legends which have been taught in Saint Nicholas and are today embraced in Santa Claus.

CHAPTER SIX
Saint Nicholas in the Context of the Church:
How the Legends and Practices Started

The adoration of Saint Nicholas is neither unique to the Medieval Church nor is it an aberration to the Church. It continues today, together with the veneration of the saints.

The adoration of Saint Nicholas has been part and parcel of the teaching of the Church throughout the ages. To understand the cult of Saint Nicholas, we need to understand it in the context of the Church which advocates the adoration, or veneration, of the saints.

The early Church, when it received its status as a legal religion, also became the state religion. Connected with this was a status as the fashionable religion to be a part of.

The great infusion of new "converts" brought with it problems. One of the problems was the lack of training and instruction that new converts received. With this lack of training came false teachings, beliefs and practices. A glaring example is the focus of this chapter.

The early Church's new converts were familiar with the gods of Greek and Roman mythology. When they entered the Church without proper or sufficient training, they maintained their former beliefs with a new veneer. No longer did they pray to Zeus, Diana, Venus, Mars, Mercury and many other "gods," but they shifted their focus to the pious, holy men that were reported as having lived godly lives and gave assistance to those in need. In this way the new converts retained what was familiar while enjoying the benefits of the popular. That the Gospel truth is lost is indeed a grave misfortune.

That it continued only exacerbates the problem.

When one compares the legends and traditions of the saints with the myths from Greek and Roman religions, it does not take long to notice some striking similarities.

Both bodies of works demand a willing suspension of disbelief. Both bodies of works employ elements of superstition. Most important, both bodies of works present a God that is distanced from the human race and has no concern or interest in what happens here on earth. It ignores the fact that it was God who sent prophets to anoint kings (1 Samuel 9 & 10;15 & 16; 1 Kings 19:15-18). It also ignores the fact that throughout the Old Testament God speaks to his people through his prophets. Our God is not removed from us, nor does he stay away. Should one doubt that God is active in and among his creation, read the following from Jesus' Sermon on the Mount:

> Therefore I say to you, do not worry about your life, what you will eat or what you will drink; nor about your body, what you will put on. Is not life more than food and the body more than clothing? Look at the birds of the air, for they neither sow nor reap nor gather into barns; yet

your heavenly Father feeds them. Are you not of more value than they?...Now if God so clothes the grass of the field, which today is, and tomorrow is thrown into the oven, will he not much more clothe you, O you of little faith? (Matthew 6:25,26,30—bold emphasis mine)

God came into the world and dwelt among us. He comes to us through the Spirit in the Word and Sacraments, creating and strengthening faith in our hearts. As the writer to the Hebrews asserts:

Therefore, since we have a great high priest who has gone through the heavens, Jesus the Son of God, let us hold firmly to the faith we profess. For we do not have a high priest who is unable to sympathize with our weaknesses, but we have one who has been tempted in every way, just as we are—yet was without sin. Let us then approach the throne of grace with confidence, so that we may receive mercy and find grace to help us in our time of need (Hebrews 4:14-16)

Even today Rome teaches the benefits of the veneration of the saints. There is no scriptural basis for this teaching. Yet the Roman Church embraces this doctrine in direct violation of the First Commandment. They attempt to make distinctions between worshiping God and adoring or venerating the saints, but it is merely a matter of semantics. The teaching and practice is deduced from a faulty interpretation and reading of Scripture together with a blind following of the Traditions of the Church. The Traditions not only include what the Church has taught and practiced for centuries, but also uses the writings of the Church Fathers as proof of doctrines. Following are several selections from Roman Catholic books written for the layman. These demonstrate that the veneration of saints is still taught as a dogma of the Roman Church:

Devotion to the Saints—Catholic Teaching

The Council of Trent has defined the Catholic teaching in regard to the invocation of the saints as follows: "The saints, who reign together with Christ, offer up their own prayers to God for men. It is good and useful suppliantly to invoke them, and to have recourse to their prayers, aid and help for obtaining benefits from God, through His Son Jesus Christ, who alone is our Redeemer and Saviour.

Those persons think impiously who deny that the saints, who enjoy eternal happiness in heaven, are to be invoked; who assert that they do not pray for men; who declare that asking them to pray for each of us in particular is idolatry, repugnant to the word of God, and opposed to the honor of the One Mediator of God and men, Christ Jesus."

A Reasonable Doctrine

Throughout the Bible the practice of asking the prayers of others is recommended. "Pray for one another, for the healing of your souls," urged St. James (5,16). Long before, God Himself had ordered Abimelech to ask Abraham's prayers: "He shall pray for thee and thou shalt live" (Gen. 20, 7, 17). Moses had interceded for the Israelites in the desert and the prayer of Job for his friends was heard. St. Paul repeatedly asked for the prayers of his brethren: "Give me the help of your prayers to God on my behalf"(Rom. 15, 30).

Remembering that the saints are the glorified members of the Church, how can it be maintained that they do not pray for men who are the militant members of the Mystical Body? St. Jerome stated the truth nearly sixteen hundred years ago: "If Apostles and martyrs, whilst still in the flesh and still needing to care for themselves, can pray for others, how much more will they pray for others after they have won their crowns, their victories, their triumphs? Moses, one man, obtains God's pardon for six hundred thousand armed men, and Stephen prays for his persecutors.

When they are with Christ, will they be less powerful? St. Paul says that two hundred and seventy-six souls were granted to his prayers, whilst they were in the ship with him. Shall he close his lips after death, and not utter a syllable for those who throughout the world have believed in his Gospel?"

With regard to the angels, it is clear from Scripture that they intercede for men: "And the angel of the Lord answered and said: O Lord of hosts, how long wilt Thou not have mercy on Jerusalem and so on the cities of Juda (sic), with which Thou hast been angry?"(Zach. 1, 12). The angel Raphael told Tobias: "When thou didst pray with tears...I offered thy prayer to the Lord" (Tob. 12,12).

> *(Author's note: The book of Tobit, from which the last paragraph originates, is an Apocryphal book which is recognized as canonical by Rome alone.)*

Christ Himself tells us that the angels have an interest in what passes on earth: "So it is, I tell you, with the angels of God; there is joy among them over one sinner that repents" (Luke 15,10). Elsewhere, He warns us against scandalizing little children for "they have angels of their own in heaven, that behold the face of My father continually" (Matt. 18,10).

If the angels pray for us, it is certain that the saints, their companions in heaven, who are united to us by grace in the supernatural organism of the Body of Christ, also do so.

The saints are filled with intense love of their fellow men for Christ's sake. They have also great power with God, because they have passed through their time of trial and are wholly pleasing to Him. Is it not reasonable, therefore, that the Church Militant should from the beginning have begged the intercession of the saints?

Beneficial Results of Honoring the Saints
Catholic devotion to Mary and the saints has been more than justified by results. Through it the true practice of religion has been fostered, in that more prayers have been offered to God than would otherwise have been. The knowledge of the intercession of Mary and the saints has encouraged Catholics of all ages to pray through them to God.

In those churches which rejected the principle of the intercession of the saints at the time of the Reformation, fewer prayers than ever have been offered to God alone. Devotion to the saints has kept the family spirit alive in the Church. Catholics are able to pray now, here on earth, to those whom they know will be their companions and friends for all eternity in heaven.

The practice of the Church in canonizing certain of her departed children has succeeded in keeping before the faithful the highest ideals of the following of Christ. The saints are the inspiration of Catholics, and those intent on advancing in the love of God delight to read the lives of the saints for their encouragement and imitation.

Moreover, the history of the Church is full of instances in which Our Lady and the saints have responded to prayers offered to them.

Almost every Catholic can relate such an instance as the result of his own personal experience. It has been proved beyond doubt that it is far better to have the angels and saints praying with us than for us to pray alone.

(Ripley: *This is the Faith*, pp. 329-331—bold emphasis mine)

The teaching of Rome clearly shows that the end justifies the means. More people are praying, thus it is a good practice to pray to the saints. There are many proofs that these saints have answered prayers and intervened on behalf of the believer. Is that a valid argument for the practice? When King Saul visited the witch of Endor and asked for the ghost of Samuel, God allowed the ghost of Samuel to appear to Saul (1 Samuel 28). Does that then mean that witchcraft, séances and spiritualistic practices are valid and God-pleasing? No. God worked through the witch of Endor to reveal to Saul what his unbelief would bring him. The arguments in support of the veneration of saints is a faulty doctrine based on suppositions of scripture that require a gigantic leap in logic.

The veneration of saints also returns the focus of man's salvation to man himself. The section in bold type above especially points out the reason for the veneration of saints—for encouragement and imitation. It is the Gospel alone that changes people's hearts and leads them to live God-pleasing lives. By ourselves we are helpless to gain salvation or to aid in our salvation.

The *Basic Catechism* also has these items about the veneration of saints:

WHAT IS A SAINT?
A saint is a holy person on earth or in heaven, especially someone who grew so close to God on earth that the Church declared him or her a saint after death.

WHAT IS A PATRON SAINT?
A patron saint is a special person to imitate and pray to for help; a heavenly protector, usually one's name saint.
(Basic Catechism, p. 70)

WHO WILL HAVE GREATER HAPPINESS IN HEAVEN?
They will have greater happiness in heaven who loved God more unselfishly on earth. (Basic Catechism, p. 77)

WHAT IS THE DIFFERENCE BETWEEN ADORATION AND VENERATION?
Adoration is the worship we give to God alone as the infinitely holy and Supreme Being. Veneration is the honor we give to the Blessed Virgin as the Mother of God, and to the angels and saints as the special friends of God.

WHY DOES THE CHURCH HONOR THE SAINTS?
The Church honors the saints (1) because they are the chosen friends of God; by honoring them, we honor God himself; (2) because, by the example of their lives, they encourage us to grow in faith, hope, and love.

WHY DOES THE CHURCH HONOR THE ANGELS?
The Church honors the angels because they constantly adore the Trinity, and because they are God's special messengers **to assist human beings on the path of salvation.** (*Basic Catechism*, p. 153—Emphasis mine).

Notice again the emphasis on personal salvation, as noted in the highlighted text above. The selections all teach the believer that the imitation of the saints and angels is the path to salvation. If anyone doubts that this doctrine is still taught and practiced today, read the classified ads of your newspaper and see how often St. Jude is thanked for an answer to prayer. Browse through almost any Christian bookstore and note how many "saint medals" and other icons may be purchased. The doctrine is alive and well and flourishes even today.

A book entitled *My Way of Life*, printed by the Confraternity of the Precious Blood, was written and published as a simplified volume of Thomas Aquinas' *Summa Theologica*. This volume is intended for the layperson in the Roman Catholic Church.

The following quotes are from this work:

> *Adoration was originally a general term which meant to pay tribute to someone's excellence. The young man who is in love says that he adores the woman of his choice. He means that he honors the virtues which she possesses. When we use the word adoration in relation to religion, the word retains this original meaning. We adore God or His saints because of the excellence of their holiness. The adoration we give to God is called latria. Latria is the honor we pay to God as the infinitely perfect being, the Creator and Lord of the universe. The adoration we pay to the saints, their relics or images, is called dulia. Dulia is the veneration we give to the saints because, through the grace of God, they have achieved real holiness and union with God in heaven. Because the Blessed Virgin Mary is the Mother of God, and because God's grace has made her the most excellent of all the saints, we pay her the tribute of hyperdulia or superveneration. The veneration which we pay to Mary or to the saints is ultimately an adoration of God Himself, because what we honor in Mary or the saints is the share in the divine life which God has generously given them* (p. 391).

The word *dulia*, as used by Paul in the New Testament, has been in the context of Paul's title as "Servant of Christ Jesus." The usage of the words "latria" and "dulia" re-inforces the contention I made earlier in this chapter. The myths of Greek and Rome as well as the legends of the saints portray before men a God who is distant from our trials and tribulations, lives and experiences. The words, as we find them in the above selection, basically tell us that we worship (latria) God but we serve (dulia) the saints. God is unapproachable, so we go instead to the saints and ask them to pray on our behalf. The saints are seen as having earned more "respect" with God, therefore their prayers would carry more weight. Yet it is a worship of what the saints have allegedly done and accomplished. This is definitely a worship of the saints which Scripture expressly forbids. The only person whose deeds we are allowed to praise and worship is the life, work and deeds of Jesus Christ, the Son of God.

Yet another selection from that book:

The virtue of observance includes the virtues of dulia—or veneration—and obedience. By dulia men bear witness to the dignity or power of other men. To praise the President of the United States, to bow to him as he passes in a parade, to erect a statue in his honor—all these are acts of the virtue of dulia. To venerate the saints by asking them to intercede with God for us is an act of dulia. It pays tribute to the spiritual dignity of the saints as the friends of God in heaven. Because the Virgin Mary is the greatest of all the saints and the Mother of God Himself, Christians pay to Mary the tribute of hyperdulia or superveneration (p. 398).

Because all the members of the Church are one in Christ, it is even possible for men to make satisfaction for the sins of others. They cannot, of course, furnish a remedy to others against future sin. One man's fast does not tame another man's body. But a man can pay the debt of punishment for another man's sin. This possibility is based on the bond of charity which makes all the members of the Church members of one family. As members of one spiritual family, they can help one another to pay the debt of sin. It is this same principle which is the foundation of the Church's practice of granting indulgences. An indulgence is the remission, in whole or in part, of the temporal punishment due to sin. It is not a forgiveness of sins, but a remission of the temporal penalty for sin.

In fact, no one can gain an indulgence unless he is in a state of grace, united with Christ in charity. Indulgences are granted from the great treasury of merits gained and satisfactions made by Christ, His Blessed Mother and the saints. They are granted by the Church to those who are living members of the Church through charity (pp. 560-561).

This selection brazenly attributes to man the ability not only to make atonement for his sin, but also for the sins of others. That is contrary to Scripture which plainly says:

I, even I, am the Lord, and apart from me there is no savior. (Isaiah 43:11)

For there is one God and one mediator between God and men, the man Christ Jesus. (1 Timothy 2:5)

No man can redeem the life of another or give to God a ransom for him—the ransom for a life is costly, no payment is ever enough--that he should live on forever and not see decay. (Psalm 49:7-9)

Salvation is found in no one else, for there is no other name under heaven given to men by which we must be saved. (Acts 4:12)

The next day John saw Jesus coming toward him and said, "Look, the Lamb of God, who takes away the sin of the world." (John 1:29)

All this is from God, who reconciled us to himself through Christ and gave us the ministry of reconciliation: that God was reconciling the world to himself in Christ, not counting men's sins against them. And he has committed to us the message of reconciliation. (2 Corinthians 5:18-19)

My dear children, I write this to you so that you will not sin. But if anybody does sin, we have one who speaks to

> the Father in our defense—Jesus Christ, the Righteous
> One. He is the atoning sacrifice for our sins, and not only
> for ours but also for the sins of the whole world. (1 John
> 2:1-2)

The Roman view therefore that we can atone for our own sins, much less for the sins of our fellow believers, is unscriptural. With this also the teaching of the merits of the saints also needs to be exposed for the pious fraud which it is. The saints themselves are saints by the blood of Christ alone, not by their deeds. Thus Scripture refutes this false Roman teaching:

> The souls of the dead are not separated from all contact with
> this world in which we live. In the ordinary providence of God,
> they cannot come to us, nor can we speak to them with the
> ease promised by spiritualists and mediums. Neither the Ouija
> board, nor spirit writing, nor table tapping is a means of
> communicating with the souls of the dead. It is possible that
> God has, on rare occasions, allowed an angel to appear to men
> in the guise of one of their relatives or friends. God may allow
> this in order that the living may be incited to pray for the dead
> or to mend their own sinful ways of life. God might even, by a
> miracle, allow a departed soul to assume the appearance of its
> own body for the same purposes. But such events are rare.
> Normally, the souls of the dead remain in their own places.
> They are in contact with us not in the sense that they can come
> to us or speak to us, but in the sense that they can know,
> through infused knowledge or through their vision of God,
> what we are doing and what is happening to us. Thus the
> saints can know that we are praying to them, asking them to
> intercede with God for us. Knowing this, they can intercede for
> us and so help us to attain our own salvation. Some
> theologians think that even the souls in purgatory can know us,
> and so can hear our prayers to them and intercede with God
> for us. Whether this be true or not, one thing is certain: the
> souls in purgatory need help, and we can give it to them (p.
> 589)

The happiness of the saints will be greater after the general judgment than before. It is true that the saints will have achieved the essential element of their happiness—the vision of God—before the judgment. But after the general resurrection and the last judgment, their bodies also will find the essence of human happiness. Or perhaps we should say, that after the resurrection, man—body and soul—will find his complete happiness. For then he will be happy as man, as a composite of both body and soul. His soul will be eternally happy in the vision of God, and his body will be happy in its immortality and in its union with a glorified soul (p. 601). (The previous selections from Farrell, Walter, O.P., S.T.M. and Healy, Martin, S.T.D.: *My Way of Life: Pocket Edition of St. Thomas—The Summa Simplified For Everyone*)

A council at Constantinople in the year 754 AD already denounced the practice of veneration, charging that "Satan had re-introduced idolatry." However, these policies were overturned at the Second Council of Nicaea in 787, restoring "the veneration—not the worship—of sacred images as a legitimate expression of Christian piety and faith" (Durant: *The Story of Civilization: The Age of Faith*, p. 427). Will Durant also opines:

Fathers and councils of the Church repeatedly explained that the images were not deities, but only reminders thereof; **the people did not care to make such distinctions** (Durant: *The Story of Civilization: The Age of Faith*, p. 426—bold emphasis mine).

Durant also describes Italian Christianity thus:

Italian Christianity was a romantic and colorful paganism, an affectionate polytheism of local and protective saints, a frank mythology of legend and miracle (Durant: *The Story of Civilization: The Age of Faith*, p. 456).

In regard to praying to the saints, the Lutheran Confessions clearly state:

Besides we also grant that the angels pray for us. For there is testimony in Zech. 1,12, where an angel prays: "O Lord of hosts, how long wilt Thou not have mercy on Jerusalem?" Although concerning the saints we concede that, just as, when alive, they pray for the Church universal in general, so in heaven they pray for the Church in general, albeit no testimony concerning the praying of the dead is extant in the Scriptures, except the dream taken from the Second Book of Maccabees, 15,14. (2 Maccabees is another Apocryphal work)

Moreover, even supposing that the saints pray for the Church ever so much, yet it does not follow that they are to be invoked; although our Confession affirms only this, that Scripture does not teach the invocation of the saints, or that we are to ask the saints for aid. But since neither a command, nor a promise, nor an example can be produced from the Scripture concerning the invocation of saints, it follows that conscience can have nothing concerning this invocation that is certain. And since prayer ought to be made from faith, how do we know that God approves this invocation? Whence do we know without the testimony of Scripture that the saints perceive the prayers of each one? Some plainly ascribe divinity to the saints, namely that they discern the silent thoughts of the minds in us. They dispute concerning morning and evening knowledge, perhaps because they doubt whether they hear us in the morning or the evening. They invent these things, not in order to treat the saints with honor, but to defend lucrative services. Nothing can be produced by the adversaries against this reasoning, that, since invocation does not have a testimony from God's Word, it cannot be affirmed that the saints understand our invocation, or, even if they understand it, that God approves it. Therefore the adversaries ought not to force us to an uncertain matter, because a prayer without faith is not prayer. For when they cite the example of the Church, it is evident that this is a new custom in the Church; for although the old prayers make mention of the saints, yet they do not invoke the saints.

Again, the adversaries not only require invocation in the worship of the saints, but also apply the merits of the saints to

44

others, and make the saints not only intercessors, but also propitiators. This is in no way to be endured. For here the honor belonging only to Christ is altogether transferred to the saints. ("Apology of the Augsburg Confession: Article XXI: Of the Invocation of Saints, 8-14," *Concordia Triglotta*, pp. 345,347)

The Apology states only a three-fold honor that is proper toward the saints: (1) thanksgiving to God because he has shown us examples of mercy, (2) the strengthening of our faith (when we see, for example, the forgiveness given to Peter after his denial) and (3) the imitation, first of faith, then of other virtues according to each Christian's calling ("Apology to the Augsburg Confession, Article XXI: Of the Invocation of Saints, 4-7," *Concordia Triglotta*, pp. 343, 345).

Scripture clearly teaches that honor is due to God alone as Isaiah writes: "I am the Lord; that is my name! I will not give my glory to another or my praise to idols" (Isaiah 42:8). Jesus speaks thus to Satan: "Worship the Lord your God, and serve him only" (Matthew 4:10).

We are also given the promise that God hears our prayers personally. As saints washed in the blood of the Lamb, we are entitled to approach the throne of grace in prayer. We need and have no other Mediator than Christ himself, whose blood cleanses us from all sin. The following passages tell us of this wonderful gift and promise:

Let us then approach the throne of grace with confidence, so that we may receive mercy and find grace to help us in our time of need. (Hebrews 4:16)

In that day you will no longer ask me anything. I tell you the truth, my Father will give you whatever you ask in my name. (John 16:23)

This is the assurance we have in approaching God: that if we ask anything according to his will, he hears us. (1 John 5:14)

The LORD is near to all who call on him, to all who call on him in truth. He fulfills the desires of those who fear him; he hears their cry and saves them. (Psalm 145:18-19)

Ask and it will be given to you; seek and you will find; knock and the door will be opened to you. (Matthew 7:7)

Thus we see that the veneration of Saint Nicholas is neither an aberration to the Medieval Church, nor is it unique. Today the cult of Saint Nicholas/Santa Claus is divided into two followings. One is the religious Saint Nicholas, the other the materialistic Santa Claus. Each camp denies any ties or resemblance to the other.

Nevertheless, both groups look to someone who is portrayed as omniscient, omnipotent and omnipresent. Both stand for work-righteousness, as the good, especially children, are rewarded and the evil punished in the collective bodies of tales.

The cult of Saint Nicholas is one of the most potent cults in the Church. At one time Nicholas stood third in frequency and intensity of worship, behind only Jesus and Mary (Ebon: *Saint Nicholas: Life and Legend*, p. 2). Thus he supersedes even the Apostles, Moses and the Prophets! Russia especially has adopted Saint Nicholas as her saint. Hundreds of churches have been dedicated to him in Russia (Ebon: *Saint Nicholas: Life and Legend*, p. 2).

As the Lutheran Confessions attest, we can also see how Saint Nicholas was used for personal gain. As seen in the previous chapter, pawnbrokers and merchants invoked the bishop and used his symbol as their own. As we look at Saint Nicholas in the various national customs, we see the myth become wrapped in the politics of the day. Even today, the image of the jolly elf-saint comes as a result of advertising and promotion.

Saint Nicholas is used as a "proof" that God is on one's side or to enter the homes and checkbooks of holiday shoppers.

Santa Claus: Is He For Your Child?

CHAPTER SEVEN
Nicholas "Earns" His Honor and Place of Veneration

As the previous chapter mentioned, the saints relieved the Greek and Roman gods of their duties when the state religion passed from that of mythology to the religion of Christianity. But this passage from mythology to saint legends wasn't easy. Nor was it immediate. In fact, some of the legends of the saints find particular saints doing battle with the gods and the followers of the mythological religion. The case is also true of Saint Nicholas. As we look at his battles, notice who he battles and how the god he battles has the same duties that Nicholas would later have attributed to him.

The goddess whom Nicholas battles is Artemis. Some of the earthly matters attributed for her safekeeping are seafarers, the harvest, protector of grain, fertility, women in childbirth, wild animals and in the care of small children.

At this point I will quote other sources to let you, the reader, gain an insight into the cult of Artemis. Then I will compare the Greek cult with the cult of Nicholas. Finally, this chapter will show that, as valiant as Nicholas is in legendary battle with Artemis, he is actually powerless in the religious struggles all around us.

Edith Hamilton, in *Mythology: Timeless Tales of Gods and Heroes*, writes about Artemis:

> ### ARTEMIS (DIANA)
> *Also called Cynthia, from her birthplace, Mount Cynthus in Delos.*
>
> *Apollo's twin sister, daughter of Zeus and Leto. She was one of the three maiden goddesses of Olympus: —*
> *Golden Aphrodite who stirs with love all creation,*
> *Cannot bend nor ensnare three hearts: the pure maiden Vesta Gray-eyed Athena who cares but for war and the arts of the craftsmen, Artemis, lover of woods and the wild chase over the mountain.*
>
> *She was the Lady of Wild Things, Huntsman-in-chief to the gods, an odd office for a woman. Like a good huntsman, she was careful to preserve the young; she was "the protectress of dewy youth" everywhere.*
>
> *Nevertheless, with one of those startling contradictions so common in mythology, she kept the Greek Fleet from sailing to Troy until they sacrificed a maiden to her. In many another story, too, she is fierce and revengeful. On the other hand, when women died a swift and painless death, they were held to have been slain by her silver arrows.*
>
> *As Phoebus was the Sun, she was the Moon, called Phoebe and Selene (Luna in Latin). Neither name originally belonged to her. Phoebe was a Titan, one of the older*

gods. So too was Selene—a moon-goddess, indeed, but not connected with Apollo. She was the sister of Helios, the sun-god with whom Apollo was confused.

In the later poets, Artemis is identified with Hecate. She is "the goddess with three forms," Selene in the sky, Artemis on earth, Hecate in the lower world and in the world above when it is wrapped in darkness.

Hecate was the Goddess of the Dark of the Moon, the black nights when the moon is hidden. She was associated with deeds of darkness, the Goddess of the Crossways, which were held to be ghostly places of evil magic. An awful divinty, Hecate of hell, Mighty to shatter every stubborn thing.

Hark! Hark! her hounds are baying through the town.
Where three roads meet, there she is standing.
It is a strange transformation from the lovely Huntress flashing through the forest, from the Moon making all beautiful with her light, from the pure Maiden-Goddess for whom Whoso is chaste of spirit utterly May gather leaves and fruits and flowers. The unchaste never.
In her is shown most vividly the uncertainty between good and evil which is apparent in every one of the divinities.

The cypress was sacred to her; and all wild animals, but especially the deer. (pp. 31-32)

Michael Stapleton writes in *The Illustrated Dictionary of Greek and Roman Mythology*:

> **ARTEMIS** *The daughter of Zeus and Leto and the twin sister of Apollo. In Homer she is Mistress of Beasts, Lady of all Wild Things, and A Lion unto Women—one of her titles is Eileithyia 'who is come to aid women in*

childbirth.' All these descriptions combine with her function in the care of small children, and seem to look back to origins in the very old, pre-Hellenic times, when the great fertility goddess of the eastern Mediterranean would have been a single deity, overseeing all the functions of fertility and motherhood which were divided among the Olympian goddesses of later times.

In keeping with the character of the Great Mother, from whom she undoubtedly derived, was the worship accorded Artemis in Ionia. Her cult centre was at the great seaport of Ephesus, where her temple was of such magnificence as to become known as one of the wonders of the world. There she was the 'giver of fertility' and the multi-breasted image of Artemis of Ephesus looks very different from the more familiar one of her as a chaste huntress. Phocaean Greeks took the cult to the west and established it at Massilia (Marseilles). From there it found its way to Rome, where it soon absorbed the cult of Diana.

From her ancient lineage Artemis kept a strange cult which had its centre in Brauron in Attica, where her votaries dressed as bears (in the story of Callisto there is a strange echo of the bear connection). There was a precinct sacred to Artemis Brauronia on the Acropolis. She was not, in Greek mythology, a goddess of the moon. Her appearance in the Iliad reflects no glory on her. In Book XXI she incurs the wrath of Hera for an ill-timed gibe at Apollo. Hera tells her that killing beasts is her proper function: but if she will try to struggle for power with her betters she had better be taught a lesson. Whereupon Hera beats her about the head with her own quiver and Artemis runs crying to her father Zeus.

Nevertheless, Artemis was a firm favourite with women, particularly with the ordinary wives and mothers who honoured her in her original form. (p. 40)

The reason that I have included these sections on Artemis is two-fold. First, some tales in the Nicholas legends find the sainted bishop, both alive and dead, do battle with the Greek goddess. Secondly, many of the attributes, duties and titles that once belonged to Artemis in mythology now belong to Saint Nicholas in the Traditions of the Church.

With this in view, there can be no way that anyone can explain the veneration of saints in general and of Nicholas in particular as anything other than idolatry.

This chapter also shows that the legends intended to show a saint as a great "Defender of the Faith." Thus his battles with Artemis of the old religion are viewed as his valiant success against paganism. I will relate one episode that shows that Nicholas is not as vigilant or as powerful as the legends and tales make him out to be.

Various legends have come down to us in bits and pieces about Nicholas' alleged battles with the Greek deity. He battled the priests while he was alive and vandalized the temple of Artemis after death. Here again, legends vary. Some report that the saint physically tore down the altar to Artemis with his own hands (possibly to support the Crusades?). Others say that the temple altar fell while or after Nicholas prayed for its removal (perhaps advocating monasticism and piety?) (Ebon: *Saint Nicholas: Life and Legend*, p. 40). That the tales differ also in when the event(s) happen (in life or after death) also reflects biases inherent in the stories. If one were to revere Nicholas as a holy man, then it is reasonable for him to do battle while living and displaying his pious actions. If one were to perpetuate and keep the cult of Nicholas alive, then it becomes imperative for the tale to portray Nicholas as active even now after death. How else could you justify invoking Nicholas for his help in prayer?

The two selections cited above reveal the same attributes given to Artemis and to Nicholas. Perhaps then the tales themselves became the justification for invoking Nicholas in the manner in which he is invoked? It would seem logical, since you could then give those honors to Saint Nick since he "earned" them.

The underlying theme is the same theme that played in the Canaanite religions which Yahweh God expressly forbid the Children of Israel to partake of. The underlying theme is one of fertility and its attendant consequences. The worship of Baal and Asherah was fertility oriented. These Canaanite practices often led the Children of Israel astray. The Canaanite religion included temple prostitution. This practice followed through in the Eastern religions and on into Greek and Roman mythology. To appease the gods, the husband was expected to be unfaithful to his wife and perform his duties with the temple prostitute. This is what Nicholas inherits with the usurption of the Artemis cult. It is given the appearance of godliness and coated with a Christian morality. Nevertheless the cult is the same as that practiced by the followers of Artemis and Diana, the Canaanite fertility gods, the Egyptian fertility god and even Native American fertility rites.

The picture of Nicholas as a vigilant defender of youth and truth, alas, finds that his vigilance is not always open-eyed. Beginning in 807 Nicholas' tomb was under attack by Moslem invaders. Merchants from the West also sought to take the bones of the saint back to their own home towns, no doubt for their benefit in the tourist trade sure to follow. A band of monks were able to ward of both Moslem attackers and Western capitalists until about 1084 AD. In 1087 the bones were guarded by only three monks.

Merchants from Bari were able to transfer the bones from Myra to Bari. The date of the completion of this transfer was May 9th—the date which the Russian Orthodox Church still observes as a feast day (McClintock and Strong: *Cyclopaedia of Biblical, Theological and Ecclesiastical Literature*, Volume VII, p. 62)!

54

The citizens of Bari, however, did not plan on just burying the bones or leaving them sit in a closet someplace. Remember, this is the third-most invoked saint in the Church! A basilica was built to house the remains so that pious Catholics could come and pray to the saint and hopefully benefit from his remains. Sparing no expense, Moslem craftsmen are hired to build and decorate the basilica. These crafty craftsmen were devious. Using ornate Arabic calligraphy, they painted the inscription inside the basilica: "THERE IS NO GOD BUT ALLAH, AND MOHAMMED IS HIS PROPHET." (Ebon: *Saint Nicholas: Life and Legend*, p. 78)

This phrase was not discovered by the church officials for several years. When it was discovered the officials decided to just leave it be so that the beauty of the script would not be disturbed. So what is Nicholas' role in this? Why was this interesting anecdote included here?

This particular story illustrates rather vividly the utter folly of the stories of Nicholas' battles with Artemis. If Nicholas is, indeed, ever vigilant, then why has he allowed that inscription to stand? Why doesn't he appear to the craftsmen and admonish them? Why doesn't he come down and remove the offensive inscription while yet leaving some essential beauty intact? The answer is that the cult of Saint Nicholas is a fraud. The sensory evidence before us shatter the myths and legends of the bishop. The practice that is in existence, despite what Rome may teach or explain about distinctions, is in essence idolatry. The myths have made Nicholas a man who became a god. Against this practice, and any teaching that leads to this practice, Scripture expressly speaks. The worship-veneration of saints is a form of Antichrist as it takes honor, glory and the work of Christ and gives it to the saint, in particular patron saints. Rome may make fine distinctions; the people never have.

Interestingly, Paul himself had a "run-in" with the cult of Artemis. In Acts 19:23- 20:1 we see the results of Paul preaching the Word of

God and its results. The underlying reason for the riot at Ephesus was not theology—it was economics!

Demetrius, a silversmith, saw his business take a nosedive after Paul started preaching. Demetrius made his living making icons of the goddess Artemis, whose temple was based in Ephesus. Did Paul vandalize the temple? No. Did Paul waste time praying for the destruction of the temple? Again, no. Paul merely preached Law and Gospel. He pointed out sin and its consequences. He preached forgiveness in the blood of the crucified and risen Lord Jesus Christ. God worked in the hearts of the Ephesian people repentance and faith.

To see that Paul and the new converts were free from blame in anything, note what the city officials say:

> *"You have brought these men here, though they have neither robbed temples nor blasphemed our goddess. If, then, Demetrius and his fellow craftsmen have a grievance against anybody, the courts are open and there are proconsuls. They can press charges. If there is anything further you want to bring up, it must be settled in a legal assembly. As it is, we are in danger of being charged with rioting because of today's events. In that case we would not be able to account for this commotion, since there is no reason for it"* (Acts 19:37-40)

Why should Nicholas resort to violence and destruction when the early Christians trusted solely in the power of God's Word? Why should Nicholas spend his time praying against the temple and its goddess when he ought to have been praying for the faith of the faithful? Why didn't Nicholas devote himself totally to preaching and teaching the Word and administering the sacraments and allowing God to work through these means of grace?

No doubt the stories of Nicholas serve to inspire the Church to be socially active. The Church must right wrongs, protect and defend the weak and rebuke tyranny. But that is not what the Church's purpose is. The Church exists to proclaim to mankind its sinfulness. The Church is placed into the world to share the Gospel of Jesus Christ. The message of the Church is to be of spiritual freedom and equality in the blood of Christ. It is when the Holy Spirit works and strengthens faith in the hearts of people that true repentance and godly living springs forth.

CHAPTER EIGHT
Saint Nicholas and Nationalism

Noting the universal appeal of Saint Nicholas, it does not surprise us then that he takes on different national flavors. Even as generations altered the myths to suit their needs and/or beliefs, even so did each nation and race of people knit a nationalistic cloak around the myths. This section looks at the various nationalistic influences into the myths and legends so that we can better see how our Santa Claus evolved to become today's jolly old elf.

ITALY
Nicholas has a rival in the form of Befana. Her role is as ambivalent as Nicholas' role. Her involvement with children is said to date back to Christ's birth. Befana missed the three Wise Men, thus she is condemned to search for them forever. Italian mothers would often invoke Befana's name in order to frighten or intimidate their children (Ebon: *Saint Nicholas: Life and Legend*, p. 78). Befana makes her travels on January 5 leaving gifts and candy to make up for the gift she failed to give to the Christ-child.

Nicholas' relics for a time rested in Bari, Italy, making Italy the center of Nicholalotry (as noted in the previous chapter).

SPAIN
The Spanish legends report the three Wise Men bringing gifts on January 5. As a seafaring nation, the Spanish people invoked and gave honor to the bishop-saint. Early Spanish explorers named new lands and ports after Nicholas. (Giblin: *The Truth About Santa Claus*, p. 22)

FRANCE
As we saw in a previous chapter, the French invoked Nicholas for help in the marriage of daughters. The French also saw Nicholas as a patron of students more so than other nations (Ebon: *Santa Claus: Life and Legend*, pp. 53-56).

In the 1200's the French began the practice of organizing and conducting Saint Nicholas Day parades. The parades started in honor of the three school boys brought back to life. The tradition had spread throughout Europe by the 1400's. Unfortunately, just as Saint Patrick celebrations have become quite disorderly today, so too had the Nick parades. Pedestrians were beaten and students had become greedy. The parades were outlawed and into the void which was created came another tradition. Schoolmasters would impersonate the saint and interview the students one by one. The schoolmaster would urge each one to be good, giving them small presents such as apples, nuts, small cakes, quill pens, etc. To those who were lazy or disobedient he gave rods. If this sounds similar to the department store/mall Santa Claus of today, you are not far from the truth. The schoolmaster, as part of his impersonation, would wear a red robe and white beard! (Giblin: *The Truth About Santa Claus*, pp. 28-30)

SWEDEN
Jultomten (Christmas empty tin) comes on December 24. *Jultomten* was an elf with a red cap who rode a sleigh pulled by *Julbock*

60

(Christmas goat). Swedish children would put out porridge for *Jultomten* and hay and carrots for *Julbock* (Giblin: *The Truth About Santa Claus*, p. 23).

RUSSIA

The related Russian legend entails one known as Baboushka. Baboushka was a witch-like old woman who had given wrong directions to the Wise Men. She was then condemned to wander around and hope to find the Christ-child, thereby gaining forgiveness (Giblin: *The Truth About Santa Claus*, p. 23).

The catalyst for the veneration of Nicholas in Russia deals with the conversion and Christian marriage of Vladimir of Kiev in 988 AD. The introduction of Christianity and Nicholas definitely had political overtones. Vladimir made his nation Christian and received baptism in order to win the hand of Anna, the daughter of the Greek Emperor, Basil II. This marriage came with part of the Crimea as a dowry (Durant: *The Story of Civilization: No. 4—The Age of Faith*, p. 536). It did not hurt that the Greek priests explained to Vladimir the divine origin and right of kings and the usefulness of this doctrine to promote order and stability (Durant: *The Story of Civilization: No. 4-- The Age of Faith*, p. 448).

Vladimir was eager to demonstrate to his new bride that his faith was genuine. First, he gave up his five wives and 800 concubines. Then he ordered that the statue of Perun, the top Slavic deity, be tied to the tail of a horse and dragged down to the Dnieper River. There the statue was beaten to pieces and thrown into the river. Then Vladimir ordered a wholesale baptism of all residents of Kiev.

However, Anna was turned off by these events. She no doubt was used to a more refined style of governing. Maybe she realized that the events were merely external actions and that no demonstration of real faith was exhibited. No one reports why Anna was upset by these events. But the widowed Empress Theophano endeavored to console her distraught cousin in Kiev. Thus she sent a note of encouragement and sympathy to Anna. With this note also came relics of Saint Nicholas (Ebon: *Saint Nicholas: Life and Legend*, p. 76). This encouragement helped Anna overcome her fears and remain in Kiev. Vladimir was also able to keep his Crimean dowry, giving Russia a valuable and viable seaport. Thus in the East, we do not see Nicholas as a caretaker and guardian of children. His patronage extends merely to sailors (Ebon: *Saint Nicholas: Life and Legend*, p. 14).

We do find another name given to Nicholas by the Russians. He is known by them as Nicholas Chudovorits (Nicholas the Wonder Worker) (Crichton: *Who Is Santa Claus? The True Story Behind A Living Legend*, p. 30)

GERMANY

The Germans had various names for Saint Nicholas: *Pelze Nicol* (Furry Nick), *Weihnachtsmann* (Christmas Man) and *Schimmelreiter* (Rider of the White Horse). *Schimmelreiter* had an assistant named *Knecht Ruprecht. Knecht Ruprecht* was armed with a switch, a sack and chains. The switch was used to whip bad children. The sack and chains was used to carry off really bad children (Crichton: *Who Is Santa Claus? The True Story Behind A Living Legend*, p. 77). Imagine the fear the children must have had at Christmastime. Again, a point which I cannot stress enough is that the legends are propelled by the Law and are devoid of the Gospel. The peace on earth to men on whom God's favor rests is absent in children if they think that something or someone is "out to get them." It also plays upon the minds of vulnerable and believing children. Such deception is inexcusable. The true Gospel message is lost; children are left with a fear of God and/or the Church. Can we justify this behavior and belief? The words of Christ in Matthew 18:6, Mark 9:42 and Luke 17:2 need to be taken to heart: "If anyone causes one of these little ones who believe in me to sin, it would be better if a millstone were tied around his neck and he were tossed into the sea."

AUSTRIA
The Austrian version had a man named *Krampus*. *Krampus* had a long, red tongue and wild demonic eyes. Again, he roamed the streets in search of bad children (Crichton: *Who Is Santa Claus? The True Story Behind A Living Legend*, p. 77).

HOLLAND
Holland is the only Protestant nation to retain Saint Nicholas after the Reformation (in name, that is. A later chapter looks at the effects of the Reformation on Saint Nick and how the cult survived). Part of Nick's persona in Holland was political, which may explain why he survived.

The Dutch were dependant upon the sea for their survival. Thus the patron saint was "needed" regardless of religious leanings. But that is only part of the story of Nicholas' enduring popularity in Holland. One must take note that at the time of the Reformation, Holland was controlled by the Hapsburg family. The Hapsburgs were based in Spain and spoke Spanish. The Hapsburgs had gained control, usually through marriage, of Holland, Austria, and the southern half of Italy as well as Spain. The Hapsburg ruler had also been elected Holy Roman Emperor. One can readily see that much of Europe would acquire a resentment of anything Spanish and friction between many European rulers and the Hapsburgs resulted. This helped the Reformation—Charles needed to keep the German princes happy to aid in defending the Turks. Many princes were more than eager to protect Reformers condemned by Rome out of spite against Charles of the Hapsburg family.

The Dutch legends of Saint Nicholas have the saint riding upon a magnificent horse on Saint Nicholas Eve. Behind him would come a man known as Black Peter. Black Peter either rode a mule or walked behind Nicholas. He carried presents and birch rods. Black Peter was, in legend, the Devil. Often Black Peter would be portrayed wearing the clothes of a sixteenth century Spanish official. He entered through the chimneys to deliver presents (Giblin: *The Truth About Santa Claus*, pp. 36-37).

The roots of the Nicholas/Black Peter legends are believed to be descended from German or Dutch mythology. In these Dutch and German myths, people were blessed by ghostly creatures who could travel up and down chimneys as swiftly as smoke (Giblin: *The Truth About Santa Claus*, p. 38). Saint Nicholas also was transformed into a Nordic magician (although some have suggested the opposite; Santa emerged from a Nordic magician) (Ebon: *Saint Nicholas: Life and Legend*, p. 87). The belief no doubt included evil spirits having the same power to go up and down the chimney.

It is interesting that Black Peter (the persona for the Devil) would have a beneficent role in Christmas! The Bible plainly states that Christmas is not an event that the Devil would want to happen. He would not want God becoming man to live a perfect life. He would not want God becoming man to overcome the Devil in trials and temptations. Ultimately, he would not want Jesus Christ to die an innocent death for the full payment of all our sins. Christmas is about this precise message. Needless to say, the Devil actually lurks in Christmas in the Law. He is behind the "better be nice" attitude for children's behavior at Christmas. He lurks behind all the legends that do nothing but instill fear and uncertainty for children as Christmas approaches.

The Dutch certainly took Nicholas with them when they explored and settled the New World. A ship would arrive at New Amsterdam (present day New York City) every December 5. This ship became known as the "Saint Nicholas Ship" (Giblin: *The Truth About Santa Claus*, p. 40). When the British defeated the Dutch, not only was the name changed to New York, but the festival was moved to Christmas. There Saint Nick became the English Father Christmas. Yet many Dutch settlers clung to the celebration of "Sinter Claes." By marriage the name soon became Santa Claus and was popular by the end of the Revolutionary War (Giblin: *The Truth About Santa Claus*, p. 41).

The importance of Saint Nicholas, or Santa Claus, to the early Dutch children of New Amsterdam/New York cannot be overlooked. An image of Santa was on the prow of the first ship to land at the colony. The first church erected within the walls of the city was named Saint Nicholas (Ebon: *Saint Nicholas: Life and Legend*, p. 88). Today's image of Santa is largely due to natives of New York. Accounts of Santa can be found in early writings such as Mrs. Schuyler van Rensselaer's *History of New York City in the Seventeenth Century* and I. N. Phelps Stokes' *Iconography of Manhattan Island* (Ebon: *Saint Nicholas: Life and Legend*, p. 89).

When the early Dutch children thought of Santa, they pictured a jolly, rose-cheeked little old man. He wore a low-crowned hat, a pair of Flemish trunk-hose and smoked a pipe of immense length. He drove a reindeer sleigh loaded with gifts from the frozen regions of the North over the roofs of New Amsterdam for the benefit of good children (Ebon: *Saint Nicholas: Life and Legend*, p. 89). We certainly can see elements of Clement Moore's poem in the Dutch description.

OTHER NATIONS
Other nations seem not to have had strong Saint Nicholas legends or traditions. Usually the gift-giving was done by a Christ-child, Wise Men, a Father Christmas or some local spirit that becomes a "Christianized" gift-giver. After the Reformation, many Protestant nations discarded the saint, but kept the traditions with new characters. From these many nations, however, we see the present day Santa Claus emerge as a hybrid of various beliefs and traditions. He definitely remains a strong and viable cult. He is also almost universally accepted by Catholic and Protestant alike. It is somewhat ironic that he has also been embraced as the universal symbol of Christmas by many who wish to have nothing to do with religion.

SANTA BECOMES MORE HUMAN
At some point in time Saint Nicholas would seem to be larger than life. At some point his persona ought to have become cold and

austere. When one looks at how "busy" this saint must be, how can little children feel that he cares about their wants and desires at Christmastime? Certainly this saint doesn't have time to play "matchmaker" for every single maiden seeking marital bliss. Nicholas couldn't possibly be able to keep an eye on every ship at sea. Yet Saint Nicholas remains as approachable today just as if he were "one of the guys." We need to see how Nicholas returned to a more human portrayal.

For this evolution of the saint also plays a vital role in the shape of today's Santa Claus.

A possible trend toward the "re-humanization" of the saint could be the medieval miracle plays. Though these plays represent the whole catalogue of the saints, the earliest of the plays were based on the Nicholas legends. In these early plays, Nicholas has an awe-inspiring personality with a touch of humor (Ebon: *Saint Nicholas: Life and Legend*, p. 57).

The saint's increasing role as patron of children no doubt kept him at a more human level. As Nicholas becomes more "involved" with children, art and plays begin portraying the theology students killed by the inn-keeper and the daughters who received their dowry as small children (Ebon: *Saint Nicholas: Life and Legend*, p. 59).

Soon Nicholas is so human (again) vagabonds begin to appeal to Saint Nicholas. Nicholas thus inherits a conflict of interests as he is invoked in some areas as the patron saint of thieves and murderers! As a more human dignitary, he could be appealed to without hesitation (Ebon: *Saint Nicholas: Life and Legend*, p. 60). In Henry IV, Part I, Nicholas is mentioned in Act II, Scene 1. Here is the exchange that displays Nicholas' new-found favor:

> Gads. Sirrah, if they meet not with Saint Nicholas' clerks,
> I'll give thee this neck.
> Cham. No. I'll none of it: I pr'ythee, keep that for the
> hangman; for I know thou worshippest Saint Nicholas as
> truly as a man of falsehood may.

(The Completed Works of Shakespeare, p. 431)

Some contrasts enter the lore of Nicholalotry. He is now patron of the murdered and murderer. He is the patron of those who make solemn oaths as well as "men of falsehood." He patronizes merchants and thieves. Today's politicians would be standing before an ethics board if they had as much conflict of interest as Nicholas appears to have.

There is a much more serious conflict of interest that is at work. The myths, legends and stories of Saint Nicholas and Santa Claus are legalistic. There is very little Gospel in the body of tales concerning this "great" man and saint. As such he stands diametrically opposed to the message and mission of the Child born in the stable in Bethlehem. This child is both God and man. This child came into the world to live a perfect life. This child would die an innocent death on the cross to pay for the sins of the world. This child doesn't tell us "you better be good, you better be nice." This child is God, who "makes His sun rise on the evil and on the good, and sends rain on the just and on the unjust" (Matthew 5:45).

Of even graver concern is the fact that through Saint Nicholas and Santa Claus the error of work-righteousness is instilled in and taught to our children. Our children grow up believing that they are rewarded (and with earthly gain!) if they do good. The Gospel offers full and free forgiveness to all who hear the Word, repent and believe that Jesus died and shed his blood to pay for all sin.

CHAPTER NINE
Saint Nicholas and the Reformation

Since we have seen how Nicholas has been part and parcel of the doctrine of the veneration of saints in the Roman Catholic and Eastern Orthodox Churches, the question naturally arises as to how Nicholas fared during the Reformation.

Nicholas had indeed received some bad press at the time of the Reformation. The following is a poem, written by Barnaby Googe, found in a book entitled *The Popish Kingdom* that was published in London in 1570:

> *Saint Nicholas money used to give maydens secretlie,*
> *Who, that he still may use his wonted liberalitie,*
> *The Mothers all their children on the Eve do cause to fast;*
> *And when they everyone at night in senseless sleep are cast,*
> *Both apples, nuttes and pears they bring, and other things beside,*
> *As caps, and shoes, and petticotes, which secretly they hide*

As in the morning found, they say, that this St. Nicholas
brought,
Thus tender mindes to worship saints and wicked things
are taught.
(Jones: *The Santa Claus Book*, p. 19)

Luther himself was not fond of the diabolical saint. He denounced Saint Nicholas' Day as a holiday "in which so much childishness and falsehood are blended" (Giblin: *The Truth About Santa Claus*, p. 30). Luther in his *Large Catechism* writes his wish that God would be thanked and praised as often and fervently as Nicholas was:

For this end it is also of service that we form the habit of
daily commending ourselves to God, with soul and body,
wife, children, servants, and all that we have, against
every need that may occur; whence also the blessing and
thanksgiving at meals, and other prayers, morning and
evening, have originated and remain in use. Likewise the
practise of children to cross themselves when anything
monstrous or terrible is seen or heard, and to exclaim:
"Lord God, protect us!" "Help, dear Lord Jesus!" etc. Thus,
too, if any one meets with unexpected good fortune,
however trivial, that he say: "God be praised and thanked;
this God has bestowed on me!" etc., as formerly the
children were accustomed to fast and pray to St. Nicholas
and other saints. This would be more pleasing
and acceptable to God than all monasticism and
Carthusian sanctity. (Luther: "The Second
Commandment," *The Large Catechism—Concordia*
Triglotta, p. 601)

Luther never addressed the problems with the saint directly in his writings. However, the references to the saint, as seen in the quote above, were never favorable. Browsing through his collective works, we present the following instances when Luther refers to Saint Nicholas:

The perverseness of the human heart is surely great. In
misfortunes and dangers there is nothing more fearful

and nothing more dejected than an ungodly person. The world seems to narrow for him; and if he could, he would force his way through mountains of bronze. But when the storm subsides, all fear is shaken off, and he reverts to type.

For example, a story is told about a sailor who was overtaken by a storm and made vows to St. Nicholas, the alleged patron saint of seafarers, that if he were saved, he would set up a silver statue for him; but when he had been saved, he did not set up even a wooden one. (*Luther's Works: Vol. 2—Lectures on Genesis Chapters 6-14*, p. 379).

God could easily give you grain and fruit without your plowing and planting. But He does not want to do so. Neither does He want your plowing and planting alone to give you grain and fruit; but you are to plow and plant and then ask His blessing and pray: "Now let God take over; now grant grain and fruit, dear Lord! Our plowing and planting will not do it. It is Thy gift." This is what we do when we teach children to fast and pray and hang up their stockings that the Christ Child or St. Nicholas may bring them presents. But if they do not pray, they will get nothing or only a switch and horse apples. (*Luther's Works: Vol. 14—Selected Psalms III*, p. 114).

Christ the Lord, the comforting Teacher and faithful Shepherd, is well aware that our heart fears and dreads Him by nature because of our sins. He knows also that the devil instigates his false teachers to intensify and magnify this delusion and to create heartbreak, when we despair of Christ and regard Him as an angry judge and jailer who always looks surly. Even though I were to torture myself to death and subject myself to severe privations, my heart would nonetheless not be satisfied. Therefore *people resort to invoking the intercession of St. Mary, St. Nicholas, and other saints. My heart will impel me to do this if I look upon Christ as a judge and jailor. And then when this, too, availed nothing—impossible as it was to help and to comfort—then they said that there was no longer either help or counsel, nothing but despair. Wherever Christ is abandoned, despair must follow; then all your works are futile, and the intercession of the saints is unreliable. This fire cannot be extinguished, neither by good works nor by the intercession of the saints. And thus the picture of Christ as a judge remains in your heart, and you must despair in the agony of death. (Luther's Works: Vol.23—Sermons on the Gospel of Saint John,* Chapters 6-8, p. 59).*

Thus we should punish bishops and spiritual dominion harder and more severely than worldly dominion for two reasons: first, because this spiritual dominion does not derive from God, for God does not know these masked people and St. Nicholas bishops,[8] because they neither teach nor perform any episcopal duties. Nor did they derive from men. They have imposed themselves on others and placed themselves into this rule against [the wish of] God and men, as is the custom of tyrants who rule only out of God's wrath. Worldly dominion derives from God's gracious order to suppress the evil and protect the godly, Romans 13[:4]. Second, worldly rule, even though it commits violence and injustice, hurts only the body and property. But spiritual dominion, whenever it is unholy and does not support God's word, is like a wolf and murderer of the soul, and it is just as though the devil himself were ruling there. That is why one should beware as much of the bishop who does not teach God's word as of the devil himself. For wherever God's word is missing, there we certainly find only the devil's teaching and the murder of souls. For without God's word the soul can neither live nor be delivered from the devil.

The footnote for the previous section states:
8Luther referred to the popular game played by students
on St. Nicholas Day, December 6. They would elect a
fellow student to be "bishop" to rule over them that day in
accordance with existing episcopal ceremonies. Even
though this masquerade had been prohibited in a bull of
Pope Gregory XII in 1407, it was quite widespread and
was frequently permitted in schools, probably to provide
an emotional outlet for medieval youth who were usually
disciplined severely. (Luther's Works: Vol. 39—Church
and Ministry I, p. 252).

The following quotation comes when Luther explains the Roman practice of referring to the sale of indulgences as "alms," as opposed to giving to the poor and needy.

...Following studiously after their faithful shepherd, his
lambs strayed about in the land with indulgences;
wherever there is a parish festival or an annual fair these
beggars gather like flies in summer and all preach the
same song, "Give to the new building, that God and the
holy lord St. Nicholas may reward you." Afterward they
go to their beer or wine, also "for God's sake." But neither
commissioners nor legates are necessary to tell us that we
should give to the needy according to God's
commandment. (Luther's Works: Vol. 45—The Christian
in Society, p. 285).

The Reformation did have an effect on Saint Nicholas, but did not eradicate the cult. As I mentioned in the previous chapter, Holland was the only Protestant nation to retain an open affection for Saint Nicholas. Other Protestant nations discarded the overt person of Saint Nicholas, but kept the legends and traditions covertly. Many of these same traditions would eventually come back into the Santa Claus cult of the United States.

The British brought back an old Roman custom to replace Saint Nicholas. Father Christmas grew out of the Roman god, Saturn, and his winter feast, Saturnalia (which was celebrated the same day that Christmas would be celebrated on—December 25).

Roman soldiers had brought the Saturnalia celebration to England in 43 AD. When the soldiers left, the celebration stayed, only to be incorporated into the Christmas celebration (Giblin: *The Truth About Santa Claus*, p.32).

Father Christmas was pictured as a gigantic man in a scarlet robe lined with fur. On his head was a crown of holly, ivy or mistletoe. Unfortunately he was a symbol of festive drinking and other holiday merriment (Giblin: *The Truth About Santa Claus*, p. 33). In the Father Christmas legends we can see how the British Christmas carols and customs have come to us.

The 12 Days of Christmas reflected the length the British celebrated the Christmas season. Saturnalia had also been celebrated for twelve days. The mistletoe, as we have seen, was part of the costume of Father Christmas. The Druids of the British Isles, however, considered it a sacred plant. It is nothing more than a parasitic weed that attached itself to certain deciduous trees. Mistletoe also has certain elements of the fertility cults. We are all well aware of the custom to kiss the young lady standing beneath the mistletoe. But to the ancient Druids there was more to the plant.

The chief would harvest it with a golden sickle. It was then used to cure illnesses, produce fertility and pacify one's enemies. The Druids believed that a kiss beneath the mistletoe symbolized the end of all grievances (——: *A Family Christmas*, p. 77). I feel that there is more than mere coincidence that the mistletoe has these Nicholatian properties. And it is more than coincidence that Father Christmas has the mistletoe as an element of his costume.

The feast of Saturnalia included much drinking. Thus the wassail bowl and eggnog come to us as Christmas customs from England.

74

The Germans retain a more religious flavor to their replacement. The Germans introduced the *Christkindl* (Christ child). Children would put out breadbaskets and plates for *Christkindl* to fill with nuts, cookies and candies. It was believed that the Christkindl traveled on the back of a pure white donkey, so small bundles of straw would also be left for the animal to eat.

As religious as the Germans made their replacement, it still embodied a legalistic philosophy. Children were given "Christ bundles." These bundles contained food, caps, scarves, mittens, dolls and small toys. It was not uncommon for this bundle to be tied to a birch rod, called a Christ rod, as a reminder to the child to be good during the coming year (Giblin: *The Truth About Santa Claus*, p. 35). Other German variations were the *Weihnachtsmann* (Christmas Man) and Kris Kringle (a variation on the name of *Christkindl*— predominantly Pennsylvania Dutch).

These personages were said to travel with frightening masked companions. These companions doled out switches and punishments to naughty children. Even today, in Austria where Saint Nick is still revered, the practice continues of Saint Nicholas appearing in parades in full bishop's regalia. He is followed by a band of *Buttenmandln*. Dressed in straw and wearing fur masks, these companions would pounce upon and squeeze the young people they met along the parade route (——:*The Reader's Digest Book of Christmas*, p. 280).

The French changed the saint's name to *Pére Noel* (Father Christmas). Again, paintings picture this character with a red robe with white trim, white beard and carrying a bag of gifts (——: *The Reader's Digest Book of Christmas*, pp. 284-285). Though the names were different, the customs and practices remained intact. The underlying false theologies were still vibrant (Ebon: *Saint Nicholas: Life and Legend*, p. 87).

In chapter six we saw how the cult of Nicholas is as much a part of the Church of Rome as the worship of any other saint. We also saw what the Lutheran Confessions had to say about this practice. Protestant nations and groups have, for the most part, discarded the practice of the veneration of saints. Yet Satan retains as his agent Saint Nicholas, or better known today as Santa Claus. Today's picture of the jolly old elf-man is even influenced by Protestant theologians here in America. This nation, which embraces a "melting pot" mindset certainly has been a successful melting pot of various Nicholas legends as well as of pagan traditions brought by various peoples into the New World. The New World certainly has given the saint a new image and renewed worship even in this skeptical age. Even parents who are dead-set against teaching their children what they see as "myths" in the Bible think nothing of letting them know and revere Santa Claus, at least while they are children. The myths of the Santa cult in themselves defy reasonable and logical explanation!

Why has Santa (St. Nicholas) remained so popular? No doubt many parents remember the "joy" he brought when they were children. Peer pressure also plays a role. What child, in his or her right mind, wants to be excluded from Santa's list? What parent wants his or her child to feel that Santa loves him or her less than a friend who receives more gifts? No parent wants his or her child to be excluded from "Santa's list." Many are just as adamant in seeing that their child's self-esteem is preserved through "Santa's" gifts as they are adamant in keeping their child away from church, and thus depriving them of true self-esteem—that they are true children of God bought through the blood of Jesus Christ!

The irony is that the saint is seen as an anti-materialistic force in a materialistic society. Martin Ebon writes:

> Saint Nicholas has thus been an image basic to human aspirations, be they religious, secular, or both. Indeed, in today's effort to revive religious vitality, the saint's figure seems well suited to the task of deepening such interests. That need not mean a return to earlier, literal requests

and prayers for intercession or miracle, but it might well mean a new infusion of ethical and mystical elements into a materialistic lifepattern (Saint Nicholas: Life and Legend, p. 3)

(The disciples of Nicholas) scorned a material, transient existence and placed their trust in the eternal (Saint Nicholas: Life and Legend, p. 14)

Saint Nicholas remained popular because he had become entwined with Christmas (owing to the proximity of his feast day with Christmas) as well as the universal appeal his legends have had. Biographies of Nicholas appear in every Christian language—Greek, Latin, Armenian, Syrian, Slav and their related tongues. Biographies have even been translated into Arabic! (Crichton: Who is Santa Claus? The True Story Behind a Living Legend, p. 26)

His popularity also comes hand in hand with the feasts that have sprung up around the worship of the saint. Natural man seeks a party—and who is better at throwing parties than Santa Claus? Santa certainly finds a home and a new identity in America. He can be made generic enough to fill visions in any child's head—Catholic, Protestant or the unchurched. He can be marketed with subtle changes. The next chapter looks at how the legends from various nations have combined to create the monster known as Santa Claus. He also receives significant influence from Americans—even Protestant theologians who would normally shy away from anything Roman Catholic!

Santa Claus: Is He For Your Child?

CHAPTER TEN
Santa in the New World

Saint Nicholas arrived in the New World through the Dutch. They brought with them their patron saint, Sinter Claes. This name would soon be Anglicized to Santa Claus, at about the time of the Revolutionary War. America has had a profound effect on the cult of the saint. In fact, our picture of Santa Claus is greatly shaped by American literature, art, and advertising.

The first ship to bring Dutch settlers to America, though named the *Goede Vrowe* (*Good Woman*), bore a figure of Saint Nicholas on its prow (Jones: *The Santa Claus Book*, p. 23). He became the patron saint of New Amsterdam (today's New York City) and the first church was named after the saint (Ebon: *Saint Nicholas: Life and Legend*, p. 88). A previous chapter (Chapter Eight) looked at the image as the early Dutch children in the New World saw him. Of his enduring popularity in the New World, especially during the Revolutionary War, Martin Ebon writes:

> Yet [St. Nicholas] does not seem to be, in its form, taken
> from the Old World. If anything, he was seen as anti-

> *British, not pro-Holland, during the Revolutionary War.*
> (*Saint Nicholas: Life and Legend*, p. 90).

It is interesting that the three men most noted for creating the bulk of the image we presently have as Santa Claus resided in New York (Ebon: *Saint Nicholas: Life and Legend*, p. 91). And of course who can overlook the editorial, "Yes, Virginia, there is a Santa Claus," published by a New York City newspaper (Ebon: *Saint Nicholas: Life and Legend*, p. 105). The patron saint has definitely been influenced by the land that claims him as its patron.

Santa was very popular among the New York Dutch. Every December 5 a ship would arrive from Holland. This ship came to be known as the "Saint Nicholas Ship" (Giblin: *The Truth About Santa Claus*, p. 40). When the British defeated Holland and took possession of the Hudson Valley, not only was the name of the city changed to New York, but the festival celebrating Nicholas was changed. The festival was moved to Christmas and Father Christmas became prominent. Nevertheless the Dutch clung to their honor of "Sinter Claes." Intermarriage between Dutch and British soon brought a hybrid of Sinter Claes and Father Christmas. By the end of the Revolutionary War his name had become Santa Claus (Giblin: *The Truth About Santa Claus*, p. 41).

To speak of the influences upon Santa Claus by the New World begins and primarily centers on three men. These three men are Washington Irving, Dr. Clement Clarke Moore and Thomas Nast (Ebon: *Saint Nicholas: Life and Legend*, p. 91). Thus we begin by looking at their contributions to the cult and studying what their significance is.

Washington Irving will always be remembered for his delightful tales about the Dutch. Who can ever forget *Rip Van Winkle*? How many of us have been spellbound by the Headless Horseman in *The Legend of Sleepy Hollow*? Irving also wrote many other tales that can be found in the Dutch pseudo-history, *Dietrick Knickerbocker's A History of New York from the Beginning of the World to the End of the*

Dutch Dynasty. In this narrative Irving gives the saint color, detail and a robustness (Ebon: *Saint Nicholas: Life and Legend*, p. 93).

Following are excerpts from Irving's book describing the Dutch patron saint:

> The ship in which these illustrious adventurers set sail was called the **Goede Vrouw**, or good woman, in compliment to the wife of the President of the West India Company, who was allowed by everybody (except her husband) to be a sweet-tempered lady—when not in liquor. It was in truth a most gallant vessel, of the most approved Dutch construction, and made by the ablest ship-carpenters of Amsterdam, who, it is well known, always model their ships after the fair forms of their countrywomen. Accordingly it had one hundred feet in the beam, one hundred feet in the keel, and one hundred feet from the bottom of the stern-post to the tafferel. Like the beauteous model, who was declared to be the greatest belle in Amsterdam, it was full in the bows, with a pair of enormous cat-heads, a copper bottom, and withal a most prodigious poop!
>
> The architect, who was somewhat of a religious man, far from decorating the ship with pagan idols, such as Jupiter, Neptune, or Hercules, (which heathenish abominations, I have no doubt, occasion the misfortunes and shipwreck of many a noble vessel,)—he, I say on the contrary, did laudably erect for a head, a goodly image of St. Nicholas, equipped with a low, broad-brimmed hat, a huge pair of Flemish trunkhose, and a pipe that reached to the end of the bowsprit. Thus gallantly furnished, the staunch ship floated sideways, like a majestic goose, out of the harbor of the great city of Amsterdam, and all the bells, that were not otherwise engaged, rang a triple bob-major on the joyful occasion.

*My great-great-grandfather remarks, that the voyage was uncommonly prosperous, for, being under the especial care of the everrevered St. Nicholas, the **Goede** seemed to be endowed with qualities unknown to common vessels.* (Irving: *Diedrich Knickerbocker's A History of New York from the Beginning of the World to the End of the Dutch Dynasty*, pp. 99-100)

On looking about them they were so transported with the excellencies of the place, that they had very little doubt the blessed St. Nicholas had guided them thither, as the very spot whereon to settle their colony. (Irving: *Diedrich Knickerbocker's A History of New York...*, p. 101)

Thus, having quietly settled themselves down, and provided for their own comfort, they bethought themselves of testifying their gratitude to the great and good St. Nicholas, for his protecting care, in guiding them to this delectable abode. To this end they built a fair and goodly chapel within the fort, which they consecrated to his name; whereupon he immediately took the town of New Amsterdam under his peculiar patronage, and he has ever since been, and I devoutly hope will ever be, the tutelar saint of this excellent city

*At this early period was instituted that pious ceremony, still religiously observed in all our ancient families of the right breed, of hanging up a stocking in the chimney on St. Nicholas eve; which stocking is always found in the morning miraculously filled; for the good St. Nicholas has ever been a great giver of gifts, particularly to children I am moreover told that there is a little legendary book, somewhere extant, written in Low Dutch, which says, that the image of this renowned saint, which whilom graced the bowsprit of the **Goede Vrouw**, was elevated in front of this chapel, in the centre of what in modern days is called the Bowling Green,—on the very spot, in fact,*

> *where he appeared in vision to Oloffe the Dreamer. And*
> *the legend further treats of divers miracles wrought by*
> *the mighty pipe which the saint held in his mouth, a whiff*
> *of which was a sovereign cure for indigestion,—an*
> *invaluable relic in this colony of brave trencher-men. As,*
> *however, in spite of the most diligent search, I cannot lay*
> *my hands upon this little book, I must confess that I*
> *entertain considerable doubt on the subject.*
>
> *Thus benignly fostered by the good St. Nicholas, the infant*
> *city thrived.* (Irving: *Diedrich Knickerbocker's A History*
> *of New York...*, pp. 150-151)

Later editions of the History bore the following account of Santa
Claus bearing gifts:

> *—and lo, the good St. Nicholas came riding over the tops*
> *of the trees, in that self-same wagon wherein he brings*
> *his yearly presents to the children.... And he lit his pipe by*
> *the fire and sat himself down and smoked.... And when St.*
> *Nicholas had smoked his pipe, he twisted it in his*
> *hatband, and laying his finger beside his nose, gave the*
> *astonished Van Kortlandt a very significant look; then,*
> *mounting his wagon, he returned over the treetops and*
> *disappeared.* (Snyder: *December 25th: The Joys of*
> *Christmas Past,* pp. 218-219).

It has also been suggested by some that Irving had created as fiction
in his *History* the lore and legend of Nicholas and the Dutch settlers.
Whether Irving used actual historical events in his pseudo-history
or these "events" were the creation of his pen is still debated by
scholars today (Snyder: *December 25th.: The Joys of Christmas Past*,
p. 219). But even as fiction, the tales betray a strong association with
the saint.

Dr. Clement Clarke Moore wrote the renowned "A Visit From St.
Nicholas."

That the poem survived at all is amazing. This theological professor wrote the poem for his ill daughter. The poem would have remained private except for a lady visitor who obtained a copy and had it printed in the *Troy Sentinel*. Dr. Moore likely had in mind a troll or a gnome-like figure. This portrayal suggests a Dutch influence as the saint comes down and goes up the chimney much as the ghostly creatures from Dutch mythology (Ebon: *Saint Nicholas: Life and Legend*, p. 98). Some have seen the poem's patron saint's model as the Dutch handyman who worked at the Moore estate. At any rate, the poem has added popularity and raised the level of Santa "knowledge" and worship (Giblin: *The Truth About Santa Claus*, p. 48).

The poem has added "information" and elements to today's Santa Claus that ought to disturb us. It brings magical elements into the story and man that charms young children. He is portrayed as the eternal giver of gifts, without limit to his generosity.

The poem also cements the relationship between Saint Nicholas and Christmas Eve. The poem, allegedly, takes place when "'Twas the night before Christmas." The person whom the children hope in and whom the narrator sees is St. Nicholas. Today this poem is even politically correct—no mention is made of the most precious of gifts that descended to us through a virgin! No mention is made of the hope that we now possess with God's gift to us through his Son. For we can hang our hope upon the Christ-child who died to pay for all of our sins. We now have visions of our heavenly home dancing in our heads. The clatter that ought to be echoed is that of the Son of God becoming flesh, not of some materialistic elf who gives gifts to children.

Dr. Moore was never particularly proud of this poem. It was intended merely as a little joke for his daughter. Unfortunately, for Dr. Moore and for children today, it was published against his wishes. A family friend, Harriet Butler from Troy, New York, saw the poem and wished a copy for herself. She submitted it as an

84

anonymous poem to the *Troy Sentinel* in 1814. The secret of authorship remained for fifteen years. Even then, when the *Sentinel* learned the identity of the author, it was not revealed to the public because Dr. Moore threatened to file suit if his identity were revealed. Instead the *Sentinel* printed the following explanation:

> *In response to many inquiries the **Sentinel** wished to state that this poem was written by a gentleman who belongs by birth and residence to the city of New York and that he is a gentleman of merit as a scholar.*

The poem was again published, anonymously, in the *New York Book of Poetry* in 1837. In 1838 Dr. Moore finally admitted authorship. Long forgotten is the fact that he wrote the first Hebrew lexicon in America (*A Compendious Lexicon of the Hebrew Language*).

Forgotten is the fact that he was the Professor of Oriental and Greek Literature at General Theological Seminary. What he is remembered for is his "hymn to Saint Nicholas" that is now a part of the cultic worship (Harvey: *'Twas the Night Before Christmas (The Rest of the Story)*).

Our image of Santa Claus certainly was shaped by the drawings of Thomas Nast. An influential illustrator, Nast gave us the donkey and elephant symbols for the political parties in America. These symbols remain to this day. Tom Nast also drew Santa Claus.

The first drawing of Santa sketched by Nast was a sketch to accompany Moore's poem in an 1863 publication, *Christmas Poems*. The success of that book led to Nast's ability to acquire a better job with *Harper's Weekly* (Snyder: *December 25th.: The Joys of Christmas Past*, p. 226).

Many of the illustrations of Santa drawn by Nast were published in *Harper's Weekly*. A new drawing would appear every year. Some of the drawings were political, such as the 1864 version that portrayed Santa wearing a star-covered jacket and striped trousers as he handed out Christmas gifts to Union soldiers (none for the Confederates?) (Giblin: *The Truth About Santa Claus*, p. 55). Timely also were the drawings of Santa at the North Pole—at the time British, Russian and Scandinavian explorers were competing to be the first in history to reach that point. From Nast we receive knowledge of Santa's residence (the North Pole), a glimpse of his workshop, his records of Children, Good and Bad and we see Santa reading and answering letters (Giblin: *The Truth About Santa Claus*, p. 56-57).

The last Nast Santa drawing to appear in Harper's was published in 1886—a family of mice tucked snugly into their beds awaiting the generous saint. *Harper's Weekly* changed its format from being a newsweekly to being a homemaker's magazine. Nast's political satire was no longer welcome, and neither was Nast. But for twenty-three years Thomas Nast gave us a peek into the "life" and "work" of the legend (Snyder: *December 25th.: The Joys of Christmas Past*, p. 227)

In 1890, Nast's drawings were published in a book entitled, *Christmas Drawings for the Human Race*. The book and its drawings became popular and established in the American mind the form and uniform of Santa—a jolly elf with a red fur-trimmed jacket with a full white beard and twinkling smile (Giblin: *The Truth About Santa Claus*, p. 58).

The problems that Nast's drawings present are grave theological problems. Santa, as a metaphor for God, is seen as far off and unapproachable. The fact that he keeps a record of good and bad children is a complete reversal of the doctrines of the Law and Gospel that the Bible clearly teaches. We are all by nature sinful and we have no merit except for the innocent blood of Christ shed to pay for all our sins. The cult of Santa Claus clearly leads to work righteousness. Yet, even if the child knows that he or she has been "bad," and still receives gifts, can that child take seriously any claims that sin must be paid for?

Finally, we need to look at another famous piece of literature about the saint. That piece is the infamous editorial, "Yes, Virginia, there is a Santa Claus," printed by the *New York Sun* on September 21, 1897. The piece was published yearly until 1949 when the *Sun* merged with the *New York World-Telegram* (Ebon: *Saint Nicholas: Life and Legend*, p. 107).

The author of the editorial was Francis Pharcellus Church, the son of a Baptist pastor. Francis Church served the *Sun* by writing theological editorials, for which he was famous.

Virginia O'Hanlon herself had other credits to her life. She went on to teach school in New York for 47 years. She also attained a doctorate. But it is her letter and its responding editorial that brought her fame and, she once remarked, was the high point of her life. By the time of her death on May 13, 1971, her letter and Francis Church's response had appeared in over 20 languages (Ebon: *Saint Nicholas: Life and Legend*, p. 108).

A closer look at the letter and the editorial is in order. Though written by a theologian, it is a theological abomination. The letter and editorial are as follows:

> *We take pleasure in answering at once and thus prominently the communication below, expressing at the same time our great gratification that its faithful author is numbered among the friends of **The Sun**:*
>
>> *Dear Editor:*
>> *I am 8 years old. Some of my little friends say there is no Santa Claus. Papa says "If you see it in **The Sun** It's so." Please tell me the truth; is there a Santa Claus?*
>
> *Virginia, your little friends are wrong. They have been affected by the skepticism of a skeptical age. They do not believe except they see.*

They think that nothing can be that is not comprehensible by their little minds.

All minds, Virginia, whether they be men's or children's, are little. In this great universe of ours, man is a mere insect, an ant, in his intellect, as compared with the boundless world about him, as measured by the intelligence capable of grasping the whole truth and knowledge.

Yes, Virginia, there is a Santa Claus. He exists as certainly as love and generosity and devotion exist, and you know that they abound and give to your life its highest beauty and joy.

Alas! How dreary would be the world if there were no Santa Claus. It would be as dreary as if there were no Virginias. There would be no childlike faith then, no poetry, no romance to make tolerable this existence. We would have no enjoyment, except in the sense and sight. The eternal light with which childhood fills the world would be extinguished.

Not believe in Santa Claus! You might as well not believe in fairies! You might get your papa to hire men to watch in all the chimnies to catch Santa Claus on Christmas Eve, but even if they did not see Santa Claus coming down, what would that prove? Nobody sees Santa Claus but that is no sign that there is no Santa Claus.

Did you ever see fairies dancing on the lawn.(sic) Of course not, but that's no proof that they are not there. Nobody can conceive or imagine all the wonders there are unseen and unseeable in the world. The most real things in the world are those that neither children nor men can see.

You may tear apart the baby's rattle and see what makes the noise inside, but there is a veil covering the unseen world which not the strongest man, nor even the united strength of all the strongest men that ever lived, could tear apart. Only faith, fancy, poetry, love, romance, can push aside that curtain and view and picture the supernal beauty and glory beyond. Is it all real? Ah, Virginia, in all this world there is nothing else real and abiding.

No Santa Claus! Thank God! he(sic) lives, and he lives forever. A thousand years from now, Virginia, nay ten times ten thousand years from now, he will continue to make glad the heart of childhood. (———: Yes, Virginia, pp. 7-19).

The editorial certainly portrays elements of faith. It portrays what faith is. But the faith in this piece is misdirected. It focuses on a figment of the collective imaginations of cultures, writers, poets and artists. It does not point the attention of one's faith to the one true God, the Triune God revealed in Holy Scripture.

The child that grows up "believing" in Santa Claus is disillusioned when the fraud is revealed. What, then, is left of that commodity called "faith?" Can there be a faith in God and heaven and hell when that "faith" is undermined by a child's betrayed trust in Santa? The editorial asserts that "he exists as certainly as love and generosity and devotion exist." Can we wonder, then, why people today will challenge us with "If there is a God, why is there suffering in the world?" when editorials such as this suggest that there is a connection?

The editorial asserts "Only faith, fancy, poetry, love, romance, can push aside that curtain and view and picture the supernal beauty and glory beyond." Can we wonder then why many today, especially in churches, treat the Bible as just another piece of literature? The editorial is telling us that it is our imagination that keeps us going day to day. Our imagination serves as a release from our everyday humdrum existence. Our imagination serves as an opiate—the same function Karl Marx asserted religion also served in the lives of people!

Yes we live in a skeptical age. But that is the fault as much of those occupying areas of trust as with our "advanced" and "technical" and "scientific" age. When our children look to us for the truth, and we string them along with myths and fables, can we realistically expect them to trust us in weightier matters? And when we compare the attributes of Santa with the attributes of the Triune God, what is the rational for explaining that while one is fictitious, the other is factual? We need to ask some serious questions before we begin (or continue) to promulgate the Santa myths with our children.

Eternal souls are at stake. The Devil plays hardball—he is not above using the imagination and trust of our children for his gain. We need to "watch and pray, that we do not fall to temptation."

America has certainly taken hold of Santa and clung to him fervently. Much has been written about what he wears, in fact. One gentleman indignantly wrote the following letter to *The New York Times*:

> *What Anarchist started the notion that Santa Claus should dress in red? When I was a boy Santa Claus, whether corporeally present at a Christmas tree or merely ideally described, always wore a fur coat, as is appropriate to his northern home and to the season, and, as stated in Moore's poem, "'Twas the Night Before Christmas," which I was trained to regard as the standard book authority on Santa Claus. Who is responsible for rigging him out in red? One would think, as a resident of the North Pole, he should wear the white fur of polar animals; but in my memory he has the black or dark brown of the principal furs of the temperate zone—more practical for coming down a chimney without showing soot than either white or red.*

Stephen T. Byington
Ballard Vale, Mass.,
Dec. 11, 1913
(Snyder: *December 25th.: The Joys of Christmas Past*, p.
231)

No doubt the two greatest influences that forced Santa to don the
red suit were a soft drink company and department stores. These
two venerable institutions have put the finishing touches on today's
jolly figure who intrudes into our Christmas.

Though Nast had first presented Santa in a red suit, it was not a
universal uniform until the 1920's. It was during that roaring decade
that the Coca-Cola Company commissioned paintings for Christmas
advertising. We are well aware of these portraits that picture a
rotund, bearded man. In fact, Coca-Cola still employs the images
even today, even down to its own line of Christmas ornaments
bearing reproductions of the paintings (Ebon: *Saint Nicholas: Life
and Legend*, p. 109).

Department stores also used the saint for advertizing purposes. J. W.
Parkinson's department store in Philadelphia is the first known
store to feature Santa. On Christmas Eve of 1841 children could
watch a "real" Criscringle descend a chimney above the door of the
store. The ploy was so successful that by 1846 Parkinson's
advertised to being "Kriss Kringle's Headquarters" (Snyder:
December 25th.: The Joys of Christmas Past, pp. 231-232).

Yet it wasn't until 1890 that the department store Santa came into
being as an entity. James Edgar, the owner of the Boston Store in
Brockton, Massachusetts, had a Santa suit made that he would wear
in his store in the afternoons when children were let out of school.
In a few days his gimmick was successful. He had his floorwalker,
Jim Grant, also wear a suit. Many from throughout New England
came to see "Santa Claus." Before the turn of the century Santa sat

on a throne as youngsters sat on his lap (Snyder: *December 25th.: The Joys of Christmas Past*, p. 232). No mention is made, however, as to the color of Mr. Edgar's Santa suit.

Santa was also enlisted in political ideologies. In the early 1900's a movement was underway and gaining popularity in restricting child labor. A belief also arose that all children deserved a happy Christmas. The Salvation Army, among others, employed "Santas" to gather money for poor families (a tactic still used today and indeed muchparodied in the press and movies) (Giblin: *The Truth About Santa Claus*, p. 65)

A department store ad campaign also provides the final element to today's Santa.

In 1939, Rudolph and his red nose made his debut hawking Montgomery Ward and Company. He was created by Robert L. May, an ad copywriter for the company. That year, 2,400,000 copies of the poem were given away free to children. 3,600,000 more copies were printed and distributed in 1946. Because of the popularity, Robert May finally obtained the copyright in 1947. He then had it published in a hard cover book.

Gene Autry recorded the chart-busting song in 1949 and the animated film was first televised in 1964 (Giblin: *The Truth About Santa Claus*, pp. 71-73). The irony? Ward's rival, Sears, Roebuck, and Co., used Rudolph for its Christmas advertising campaign in 1998!

Children for decades have sent letters to Santa. Yet they ended up in Dead Letter Offices until 1914 when the Santa Claus Association was founded to answer these letters.

Should a letter come from a child that appeared unlikely to have his or her wish fulfilled by Santa, such gifts were supplied from the Association's warehouses. New Yorkers willingly contributed (Giblin: *The Truth About Santa Claus*, p. 67).

Unfortunately, Federal Postal officials were called upon to
investigate in 1928.

What followed was a severe criticism of the business practices of the
Association that betrayed the public trust. No more letters were
turned over to the Association, but postal workers took up the task.
Today municipalities, such as Santa Claus, Indiana, diligently answer
all of Santa's mail—all in order to keep alive the belief in the myth
that helps many in financial gain (Giblin: *The Truth About Santa
Claus*, p. 68).

The presence of Santa Claus in the New World, in a sense, is a real
presence. As a result of the uproar when the Vatican left St. Nicholas'
Day off of the official church calendar in 1970, the relics were
transferred from Bari, Italy, to New York City. Some of these relics
were transferred to the Greek Orthodox Church in New York City.
But the vast majority of the relics were laid to rest at the Shrine of
Saint Nicholas in Flushing, New York. This arrangement was agreed
upon by Pope Paul VI and Greek Orthodox Archbishop Iakovos
(Ebon: *Saint Nicholas: Life and Legend*, p. 80).

The New World, the United States, and the capitalistic system have
certainly embraced, used, and exploited the "saint." It is unfortunate
that this comes at the expense of the true Gospel message of the
Christ child whose birth we celebrate at Christmas. This Gospel
message proclaims that the Son of God became flesh, dwelt for
awhile among us, lived under the Law which he established,
ultimately to fulfill and keep the Law to perfection. This perfect life
would lead into the innocent death suffered by our Lord which
would shed the blood of an innocent man—the price God demanded
for payment for all of our sins. The Gospel contains no threats. It
doesn't offer hope in some vague entity that occupies our minds in
childhood only to be replaced by "grownup" matters. It offers the
only real solution to a very real problem—salvation for all from sin.

CHAPTER ELEVEN
Saint Nick and Santa Today

Today's Santa bears little resemblance to the figures and dimensions of Saint Nicholas of old and the Santa Claus of early Americana. He has become larger around the waistline, sporting a full beard and red suit. He no longer wears a bishop's garb.

Today's Santa is seen, by and large, as having no part of the church. Increasingly he is becoming more of our Christmas focus as the separation of church and state is a matter of hot civil liberties debates. Where municipalities once displayed manger scenes, Santa is now becoming more and more visible. A look is in order at how Santa is viewed and seen today.

Santa is not lost as a viable marketing tool. True, individual stores may not hire Santas today as may have been the case in years past. But malls usually have an elaborate "village" set up with Santa's throne and hours posted when Santa is available for requests (and when he is not present, the children are told that he is "feeding the reindeer"). Santa is a holiday drawing card for the mall and its merchants. What parent won't take his or her offspring to visit with the kind gentleman who listens to requests ("prayers")?

Santa is omnipresent also on the airwaves. His voice and jolly "Ho-ho-ho!" come through on multitudes of ads on the radio. We see him on television ads as he hawks products from televisions to shavers to soft drinks. We see him in newspapers and magazines as his countenance peers at us and urges us to buy the particular product that the advertiser wants plugged. Even as I write these words images come to mind of a multitude of goods and services that have been endorsed by that jolly old elf. I am confident that the reader can also remember many of these images.

Santa today is also a figure that preaches work-righteousness. The standard greeting of a department store/mall Santa is: "Have you been a good little boy/girl this year?" The implication is that if you weren't good this year, how could you expect to get anything from this kind person. All the traps of work righteousness are embodied in the Santa myth. Here let us look at the traps and how Satan uses these traps.

"I try my best"
Many today recognize that they cannot keep the Law of God perfectly. But they rationalize that God must credit them with an honest effort. In Santa they can play out their "I tried" line and be rewarded. Isn't that all Santa really asks of them? But is that what God asks?

The Bible clearly states that God demands perfection (All passages in the New King James Version):

> *Therefore you shall be careful to do as the LORD your God has commanded you; you shall not turn aside to the right hand or to the left.* (Deuteronomy 5:32)

You shall diligently keep the commandments of the LORD your God, His testimonies, and His statutes which he has commanded you. (Deuteronomy 6:17)

Therefore you shall keep the commandments, the statutes, and the judgments which I command you today, to observe them. (Deuteronomy 7:11)

Therefore you shall keep the commandments of the LORD your God, to walk in his ways and to fear him. (Deuteronomy 8:6)

And now, Israel, what does the LORD your God require of you, but to fear the LORD your God, to walk in all his ways and to love him, to serve the LORD your God with all your heart and with all your soul, and to keep the commandments of the LORD and his statutes which I command you today for your good? Indeed heaven and the highest heavens belong to the LORD your God, also the earth with all that is in it. (Deuteronomy 10:12-14)

Therefore you shall love the LORD your God, and keep his charge, His statutes, His judgments, and His commandments always. (Deuteronomy 11:1)

Therefore you shall obey the voice of the LORD your God, and observe His commandments and His statutes which I command you today. (Deuteronomy 27:10)

Cursed is everyone who does not continue in all things which are written in the book of the law, to do them. (Deuteronomy 27:26; Galatians 3:10)

Therefore you shall be perfect, just as your Father in heaven is perfect. (Matthew 5:48)

97

> *And I testify again to every man who becomes*
> *circumcised that he is a debtor to keep the whole law.*
> (Galatians 5:3)

God indeed demands perfection. If we are to abide by a certain code of conduct for salvation, then every aspect, every deed, every word and every thought in our lives, every day, hour and minute, is to be a perfect reflection of God. Yet we all realize that this is impossible. Paul reminds us in his letter to the Roman Christians:

> *Therefore, just as through one man sin entered the world,*
> *and death through sin, and thus death spread to all men,*
> *because all sinned.* (Romans 5:12)

The belief fostered in Santa that we only have to "try our best" is unscriptural. God demands perfection. Needless to say, none of us can match that goal. We daily sin much and fall short of God's demands for perfection. How, then, can we be saved? We can be saved only through the blood of Christ, shed as payment for our sins. This innocent blood washes us clean in the sight of God. God freely gives us blessings and salvation. Santa only promises them when we are good.

"I'm better than..."

We often like to compare ourselves to others. This is especially true in our sanctified life. We reason that we cannot be so bad as many of the other people around us in the world. The same is true with Santa. The good get toys and goodies; the evil get lumps of coal, rods and threats. This belief has existed as long as Saint Nicholas and Santa have been revered.

Yet what happens when those we view as "evil" also get good things, or "worse yet," better things than we get? Can Santa really be just? We soon have a mindset that "Santa" never really punishes anyone. God, who is just as loving, wouldn't punish anyone either.

But God does promise to punish, else he wouldn't be a just God. He punishes people when they rely on their "works." He punished his Son so that by faith our sins are no longer charged against us.

Can we equate faith in Santa to faith in God?

This may seem like an absurd question for a Christian to ask. Most Christians whom I know that play the Santa game with their children confess that Santa is only a figment of imagination but that God exists. But this is a question we need to study closely.

When I grew up, my parents also told me about Santa Claus. I am not ready to condemn them for their actions; their parents no doubt did the same as did their parents before them. Understand this: the cult of St. Nick/Santa is very old and very much a part of our traditions and our Christmases.

In my case, the "awful realization" that there really was no Santa Claus was not faith shattering. I continued to go to church, attend Lutheran schools and go through the seminary. In my mind Santa and God had been kept separate. But that was by God's grace.

When I gave a presentation to the Ladies Aid at St. John's Lutheran Church in Burlington, Wisconsin, on the subject of Santa Claus, no one in the group really had given much thought whether Santa could or could not undermine faith. But again, these were people who were faithful in their spiritual diets. By the grace of God these dear ladies had kept separate, in their minds, fact from fiction.

In the workplace I found an altogether different scenario. Here in this arena I found skeptics, not only of Santa, but also of the church and God. In the minds of various people were common beliefs that Santa was nothing more than a fancy child's game played when these people were children. When they grew up, they knew better. They often saw Church and God in the same light. And if their parents (and sometimes even their Church) played the "Santa game" with them, then the Bible was just another collection of tales that had amusing anecdotes and some lessons, but was not to be taken at face value.

That this scenario existed is indeed sad. For these people no doubt despaired at a legalistic situation that they felt existed in their church body. The futility of this legalistic code drove many to despair. Thus when they discovered that there really was no Santa Claus and there were no elves and that there was no record of good children and bad children, the logical and easy choice would be to hold the Bible and God in the same light of skepticism.

Unfortunately, many of these people with whom I was led to witness to refused to believe much of what the Bible said about sin and grace. They felt that a person was okay if he or she just tried to do his or her best. They could not, or would not, believe that God would give up his own Son to pay for our sins. The "opinion of the law" that is inherent in all people told these people that our sins can't just be erased that easily. They felt that a person must do something to help with his or her salvation.

It is sad that the Gospel message was hindered from shining brightly to these souls. Can we blame Santa totally for these developments? Certainly Satan is using Santa as a very effective agent in his fight. We can never underestimate the power of Satan and what he can do in our lives and in the lives of our children. By fostering the Santa of legalism in our children, we are nurturing in them a work-righteousness and building a wall that can become a barrier to the Gospel.

Is it merely coincidence that God and Santa look alike?

What is the picture that comes to your mind when you try to picture God? Many picture an elderly, kind and loving grandfather. Doesn't Santa evoke the same picture—one of an elderly, kind and loving grandfather? I see an interesting twist in these portrayals of God and Santa.

The most prominent twist is: Why do these figures receive pictures in our "mind's eye" as being "grandfatherly?" For what do you remember your grandfather? Many of us remember our grandfathers as being supportive, loving, accepting as we are, wont to spoil us and not too strict with discipline. Our grandfathers are generally loving and kind souls. They are much unlike our fathers, whom many of us remember as disciplinarians.

But God is our Father, not our grandfather.

By picturing God and Santa as "grandfathers" we take away many of the facets of our Creator. We have blotted out from our picture of God the fact that he has established codes of conduct and morality. We have obliterated any hint that sin must be punished. We have a picture of someone who has no anger. Yet God possesses these attributes as well as being our "Dad." Our grandfatherly portrait often leaves out the discipline, which a Father must surely administer to his children if they are to grow up to be decent, law-abiding citizens. God as our Father also administers discipline for our eternal benefit.

These are some things that we need to keep in mind as we consider whether or not to play the "Santa game" with our children. Do we really want to risk the faith of our children? Are the potential or alleged virtues of Saint Nicholas worth keeping alive these traditions? That is a question for each Christian to make, based on faithful study of God's word, prayer and with a lot of thought.

Santa Claus: Is He For Your Child?

CHAPTER TWELVE
Is Santa an Anti-Christ?

One question which I wish to address is this: Can we consider Santa Claus (or St. Nicholas) an Anti-Christ in the Church? Is this "harmless" elf and benefactor of children really evil incarnate (or evil planted subliminally)? To answer this question, we must first look at what Scripture says about the Anti-Christ. Then we need to compare the descriptions in Scripture to our friend from the North Pole.

Throughout the history of the Church there have been many ideas and theories about the Anti-Christ. Earliest Christians looked at the Roman empire, or the emperor in Rome himself, as the Anti-Christ. Many in Luther's day viewed the Moslems as the Anti-Christ. In our own century many held up the Soviet Union as the Anti-Christ. Historically, the Anti-Christ was seen by many as a force outside of the Church and overtly against Christ and the Christian Church. Yet when we study what the Prophets and Apostles say about the subject, we see an entirely different picture. Daniel, Paul and John all describe the Anti-Christ as *within* the structure of the Church (or the "nation of Israel"). Let us look at the descriptions of the Anti-Christ, beginning with Daniel:

> *The king will do as he pleases. He will exalt and magnify himself above every god and will say unheard-of things against the God of gods. He will be successful until the time of wrath is completed, for what has been determined must take place. He will show no regard for the gods of his fathers or for the one desired by women, nor will he regard any god, but will exalt himself above them all. Instead of them, he will honor a god of fortresses; a god unknown to his fathers he will honor with gold and silver, with precious stones and costly gifts. He will attack the mightiest fortresses with the help of a foreign god and will greatly honor those who acknowledge him. He will make them rulers over many people and will distribute the land at a price.* (Daniel 11:36-39)

St. Paul writes about the Anti-Christ ("The Man of Lawlessness"):

> *Concerning the coming of our Lord Jesus Christ and our being gathered to him, we ask you, brothers, not to become easily unsettled or alarmed by some prophecy, report or letter supposed to have come from us, saying that the day of the Lord has already come. Don't let anyone deceive you in any way, for that day will not come until the rebellion occurs and the man of lawlessness is revealed, the man doomed to destruction. He will oppose and will exalt himself over everything that is called God or is worshiped, so that he sets himself up in God's temple, proclaiming to be God.*

> *Don't you remember that when I was with you I used to tell you these things? And now you know what is holding him back, so that he may be revealed at the proper time. For the secret power of lawlessness is already at work; but the one who now holds it back will continue to do so*

till he is taken out of the way. And then the lawless one will be revealed, whom the Lord Jesus will overthrow with the breath of his mouth and destroy by the splendor of his coming. The coming of the lawless one will be in accordance with the work of Satan displayed in all kinds of counterfeit miracles, signs and wonders, and in every sort of evil that deceives those who are perishing. They perish because they refused to love the truth and so be saved. For this reason God sends them a powerful delusion so that they will believe the lie, and so that all will be condemned who have not believed the truth but have delighted in wickedness. (2 Thessalonians 2:1-12)

St. John is the only writer to use the term "Anti-Christ." In the Greek, it means "in the place of the Christ (the Annointed One)." It is this basic meaning in the Greek that we will study when we compare Santa with the descriptions of the Anti-Christ. In his epistles John writes:

Dear children, this is the last hour; and as you have heard that the antichrist is coming, even now many antichrists have come. This is how we know it is the last hour. They went out from us, but they did not really belong to us. For if they had belonged to us, they would have remained with us; but their going showed that none of them belonged to us. But you have an anointing from the Holy One, and all of you know the truth. I do not write to you because you do not know the truth, but because you do know it and because no lie comes from the truth. Who is the liar? It is the man who denies that Jesus is the Christ. Such a man is the antichrist—he denies the Father and the Son. No one who denies the Son has the Father; whoever acknowledges the Son has the Father also. (1 John 2:18-23)

Dear friends, do not believe every spirit, but test the spirits to see whether they are from God, because many false prophets have gone out into the world. This is how you can recognize the Spirit of God: Every spirit that acknowledges that Jesus Christ has come in the flesh is from God, but every spirit that does not acknowledge Jesus is not from God.

This is the spirit of the antichrist, which you have heard is coming and even now is already in the world. (1 John 4:1-3)

Many deceivers, who do not acknowledge Jesus Christ as coming in the flesh, have gone out into the world. Any such person is the deceiver and the antichrist. Watch out that you do not lose what you have worked for, but that you may be rewarded fully. Anyone who runs ahead and does not continue in the teaching of Christ does not have God; whoever continues in the teaching has both the Father and the Son. If anyone comes to you and does not bring this teaching, do not take him into your house or welcome him. Anyone who welcomes him shares in his wicked work. (2 John 7-11)

These are the passages that the authors of the Lutheran Confessions used in describing the anti-Christ. In the Apology to the Augsburg Confession, in speaking about the papacy, Melanchthon wrote:

Thus the Papacy also will be a part of the kingdom of the Antichrist if it thus defends human services as justifying. For the honor is taken away from Christ when they teach that we are not justified gratuitously by faith, for Christ's sake, but by such services; especially when they teach that such services are not only useful for justification, but are also necessary, as they hold above in Art. VII (Of the Number and Use of the Sacraments), where they condemn us for saying that unto true unity of the Church it is not necessary that rites instituted by men should everywhere be alike. Daniel 11:38 indicates that new human services will be the very form and constitution of the kingdom of

Antichrist. For he says thus: but in his estate shall he honor the god of forces; and a god whom his fathers knew not shall he honor with gold and silver and precious stones. Here he describes new services, because he says that such a god shall be worshiped as the fathers were ignorant of. For although the holy Fathers themselves had both rites and traditions, yet they did not hold that these matters are useful or necessary for justification; they did not obscure the glory and office of Christ, but taught that we are justified by faith for Christ's sake, and not for the sake of these human services. (Concordia Triglotta, pp 319, 321 (19)).*

For Paul also predicts, 2 Thessalonians 2:4, that Antichrist will sit in the temple of God, i.e., he will rule and bear office in the Church. (Concordia Triglotta, p. 227 (4)).*

The Smalcald Articles also speak of the Anti-Christ:
For Paul, 2 Thessalonians 2ff., in describing to the Thessalonians Antichrist, calls him "an adversary of Christ, who opposeth and exalteth himself above all that is called God, or that is worshiped, so that he as God sitteth in the temple of God." He speaks therefore of one ruling in the Church, not of heathen kings, and he calls this one the adversary of Christ, because he will devise doctrine conflicting with the Gospel, and will assume to himself divine authority. (Concordia Triglotta, p. 515 (39)).*

The Fathers of the Lutheran Church and the authors of its confessions hold to specific beliefs about the Anti-Christ. They point out that the Anti-Christ comes from the Church, and in fact ruling from an office within the Church. The doctrine, teaching, and practice is contrary to that of Christ and the Gospels. The Confessors also point out the vast power of the Anti-Christ. This power is not only a political power, but also a power over thoughts, beliefs, and ideas. It is the power to shape opinion. Keep these thoughts in mind as you compare the doctrines of Santa Claus with the doctrines of the Anti-Christ.

Although we do not view Santa (St. Nicholas) as an office-holder in the Church, he does occupy a prominent place. Remember, in a previous chapter we discovered that at one time Saint Nicholas ranked third in adoration behind only Jesus and the Virgin Mary. Nicholas had superseded Abraham, Moses and the Twelve Apostles! How, exactly, did Nicholas "gain" this honor?

The honor goes back before canonization. In order for someone to be canonized as a saint in the Roman Church, that person had to be more than just a good, dead Christian. The prospective saint must "prove" that he deserves that honor. That can only be proven through the use of miracles. A prospective saint is able to perform miracles because he or she has done so many good works and lived such a pristine life (see how monasticism became popular?). The miracles that were then performed became known as "works of supererogation." Simply put, these people allegedly went "above and beyond the call of duty for a Christian." These works of supererogation then went into a so-called "treasure chest of merits." It is from this chest that the Pope in Luther's day claimed he dipped from in order to print and sell indulgences. These "saints" could also draw from this "chest" in order to answer cries for help. This is where canonization takes place.

The canonization occurs after a particular deceased performed several postmortem miracles. These miracles had to be a direct answer to someone's plea (such as "Nicholas of Myra, please find a mate for my daughter"). They then had to be verified (the daughter had no suitors when suddenly Mr. Right came along and the young miss was a bride within months). The more widespread the miracles, the more authentic the now-dead person's claim to sainthood.

108

As we have seen in previous chapters, the saints in the Roman Church occupy a lofty and exalted place in the Church. It is to the saints that parishioners turn when in need or seeking a favor. The eyes of many see the saints as the agents who "get things done." This status gives to the saints an unofficial office. As such, the body of works concerning deeds, miracles, bravery and lifestyle soon bear the model after which the good Roman Catholic will strive to live the "right" life. Though dead, these saints still rule the thoughts, lives and beliefs of the people who venerate (i.e. worship) them. As one of the most venerated saints, Nicholas certainly has an office within the Church from which he rules.

The teachings of Santa Claus (St. Nicholas) are also opposed to the teachings of Christ, thus placing him "in the place (anti) of Christ." The Gospel of Christ offers full and free forgiveness. Santa offers gifts to only "good little boys and girls." The Gospel of Christ is based on the Cornerstone which God chose and the blood shed by the Lamb as payment for all sins. Santa changes his myths from culture to culture, much like shifting sand. Santa veneration is also based on man's own attempt at atonement for sin.

That man can ever atone for sin we know is hopeless. Read any epistle from Paul and the Apostle reiterates that fact over and over again. Christ is very much with us, his presence, his Word and in his Sacraments. Santa stays put at the North Pole (or wherever he resides for any particular culture). He only comes on Christmas Eve (or December at the behest of merchants). The Saint Nicholas of old came only when called upon, whereas Christ promises to be with us always, to take care of our every, basic daily need.

Finally, Christ has solved our greatest problem—sin! Santa leaves us each year to struggle anew with our imperfections for another year (and hopefully we can do well enough to be considered "good"). Santa also possesses immense power. How many children each year look forward to Santa? How many children laboriously toil over letters in the hopes of convincing Santa to grant them their wish? He has influenced the minds, beliefs, attitudes and actions of many thousands over 14 centuries in numerous countries. French maidens, Dutch and Mediterranean sailors as well as countless children, students, merchants and thieves have sought counsel and blessings from the saint. They have erected churches and cathedrals and named ports and towns in his honor. Unfortunately, the greatest influence is also the most diabolical—leading little children to believe that they can "earn" something by being good, or at least trying. That is the saddest result of all in the tragedy of this myth.

In today's day and age, as with many days and ages, the concept of the Anti-Christ ought not to be confined solely to the papacy. The papacy is the foremost Anti-Christ, but there are other institutions and beliefs and leaders who extol the virtues of those beliefs that also constitute the Anti-Christ, whether it is the Church Growth Movement, Televangelism, or Santa Claus. The Apostles warn us to watch out for them.

We ought to diligently mark them, know them and avoid them.

CHAPTER THIRTEEN
Is Santa Worship a form of Idolatry?

Another aspect of "Santolatry" to consider is whether we can consider Santa Claus an idol. By casting him in the light of the Anti-Christ we have already done that, but there is more to idolatry. The Anti-Christ will not endanger all who come under its influence. The Anti-Christ still uses the Word and Sacraments, although it uses them in a false and perverted manner. Where the Word and Sacraments are used and administered, Christ promises to be there among his means of grace. However, the cult of Santa Claus does not use the means of grace but looks to "supernatural means" to solve mankind's problems or fulfill its desires. It can also drive many away from the open and inviting arms of their Savior. By setting up and maintaining an impossible legal code, it drives many to despair and, finally, to reason that if Santa isn't real, then the Church and the Bible cannot be real either. Herein we will look at idolatry and how Santa fits in with other idolatrous practices.

God strongly forbids mankind to worship anyone other than the Creator. To the Israelites he stated:

> *I am the LORD your God, who brought you out of Egypt,*
> *out of the land of slavery. You shall have no other gods*
> *before me. You shall not make for yourself an idol in the*
> *form of anything in heaven above or on the earth beneath*
> *or in the waters below. You shall not bow down to them*
> *or worship them; for I, the LORD your God, am a jealous*
> *God, punishing the children for the sin of the fathers to*
> *the third and fourth generation of those who hate me, but*
> *showing love to a thousand generations of those who love*
> *me and keep my commandments (Exodus 20:2-6).*

God has also stated who he is and what he expects from his creation:
> *I am the LORD; that is my name! I will not give my glory to*
> *another or my praise to idols.* (Isaiah 42:8)

God also specifically states who he is and what he does. By this activity we are to know him:
> *Then all mankind will know that I, the LORD, am your*
> *Savior, your Redeemer, the Mighty One of Jacob.* (Isaiah 49:26)
> *(Note: the New International Version denotes the*
> *tetragrammaton with the word "Lord" in upper case*
> *letters. The tetragrammaton is the four-letter word in*
> *Hebrew which denoted the proper name of the Triune*
> *Creator God. Scholars believe that the Hebrew word was*
> *most likely pronounced "Yahweh.")*

Idolatry is not restricted to just bowing down before a wooden or stone statue or praying to a childish, self-serving god or goddess of mythology. Anything or anyone that takes away from one's total devotion to the true Triune God and to his message is a form of idolatry. The Triune God has revealed his identity, what he has done and still does, how he views mankind and, most importantly, his message to us. Anything or anyone that denies any of these facts that the true God has revealed to us is idolatry.

In Santa we see many of the attributes (glories) that belong to God alone. Reuel Schulz, in his book *Idols—Dead or Alive?,* addresses this very topic. He quotes a *Christian News* writer who spoke out against Santa:

I Believe in...Santa Claus?

Santa Claus a God-substitute? Listen again to the popular song that children sing each Christmas:

> *You better watch out, you better not cry,*
> *Better not pout, I'm telling you why—*
> *Santa Claus is coming to town!*
> *He's making a list and checking it twice,*
> *Gonna find out who's naughty and nice*
> *Santa Claus is coming to town!*
> *He sees you when you're sleeping,*
> *He knows when you're awake,*
> *He knows if you've been bad or good*
> *So be good for goodness' sake!*
> *Oh! You better watch out, you better not cry,*
> *Better not pout, I'm telling you why--*
> *Santa Claus is coming to town!*

Now think about the Santa myth in general and this song in particular in the light of the attributes of God. Here is a partial listing:

1. GOD IS HOLY—This means that God is distinct from all of His creatures. He is a unique being; there is nothing in heaven, on the earth, or under the earth that is like God. So is the imaginary Santa Claus.

There is no other being in the universe like him. He may go by different names in different countries, but there are no other Santa Clauses—only one. He is unique.

2. GOD IS ETERNAL—*So is the imaginary Santa Claus. He has no beginning (Who were his parents? Where was he born?), and he will presumably have no end.*

3. GOD IS UNCHANGEABLE—*Santa Claus hasn't aged a day since I was a child. He still looks the same and he still does the same things he has always done. He appears to be a changeless being, like God.*

4. GOD IS OMNISCIENT—*So is the imaginary Santa. "He sees you when you're sleeping, He knows when you're awake, He knows if you've been bad or good..." That sounds a lot like what David says about Jehovah in Psalm 139: "O LORD, Thou hast searched me and known me. Thou dost know when I sit down and when I rise up; Thou dost understand my thought from afar." (KJV)*

5. GOD IS OMNIPOTENT—*Is there anything that Santa Claus can't do at Christmas? The parents who maintain the myth may not be able to afford the expensive toy their child wanted, but that's no defect in Santa.*

6. GOD IS OMNIPRESENT—*Santa is not exactly omnipresent—everywhere at the same time. We all know that he spends most of his time at the North Pole. But somehow from that vantage point his eyes peer out over the whole earth watching children day and night without any rest. As Christmas approaches, he can be found in every department store in the city, and on Christmas Eve he manages to travel the whole world over, leaving presents at every house. Even with our space-age technology, that's quite an accomplishment. While that's not quite the same thing as being omnipresent, it certainly is close.*

7. GOD IS SOVEREIGN—*So is Santa Claus. To whom is Santa responsible? Is there anyone who has authority over him?*

8. GOD IS GOOD—*Santa also reveals his character by doing good unto others. His whole purpose is to give gifts unto men.*

9. GOD IS JUST—*So is His mythical substitute. "You better watch out, you better not cry, Better not pout, I'm telling you why—" Santa Claus is coming to town, and he's coming in the character of a judge. Children who have been good during the year will receive presents as their reward. But children who have been bad can expect stockings filled with cinders and ashes. Santa Claus, then, is the judge over boys and girls, and they had better live their lives in a way that is pleasing to him.*

10. GOD IS RIGHTEOUS—*Has anybody ever found fault with Santa Claus? Are there any moral imperfections in his character or conduct? Has he ever needed to confess his sins to anybody else?*

Well, perhaps the Santa myth is not so innocuous after all. In all of these things Santa Claus is a children's substitute for the living God.

But can it really be harmful to let our children believe in a myth?

INDEED IT CAN! And in several ways. Let me explain. First, if Santa Claus is a God-substitute for the pre-school generation, then what do young boys and girls learn about Deity during the highly impressionable years of early childhood? In an excellent article published some years ago (December 3, 1971) in "Christianity Today" Samuel Mateer argued convincingly that Santa Claus is a reflection of the secular man's concept of God. As a child accepts Santa to be his judge, he will also accept all or some of the following ideas:

1. Acceptance with God—*"He's making a list and checking it twice, Gonna find out who's naughty and nice..." The child soon learns that he can be acceptable to Santa by being "nice." Being nice guarantees rewards; being naughty means cinders and ashes. The way to be acceptable in God's sight is to do your very best. Sound familiar?*

2. God's Word—*The child knows that Santa has promised blessing upon niceness and cursing upon naughtiness. As Christmas approaches he is continually reminded of his own behavior. He has not been perfect throughout the past year, and he knows it. In fact, he has had some spells of nastiness while out shopping with his parents. But, he reasons within himself, everything will be OK. He's never known a kid yet who got cinders and ashes from Santa Claus. Nothing that he's done is bad enough for that. And Christmas morning, just as he expects, his faith in his own goodness is rewarded again. He's OK just as he is—his behavior though not perfect, is acceptable. And all this talk about cinders and ashes is just talk. Whatever God says, and whatever the child does, in the end God will reward everybody anyway.*

3. God's interest and involvement—*Santa watches his people from a distance 364 days a year, but he only visits them once—and then only when they're asleep. They can write to him at the North Pole, but he never answers their letters. Though he has a host of "angels" (elves) who assist him in his work, they generally stay at the North Pole and have little contact with children. Santa is not* *really interested in the whole life of the child, and certainly is not in a position to help him with his problems.*

God is seen as a friendly old man with a long white beard who generally stays aloof from the world but occasionally checks on it to make sure it's still running.

***4. The child's faith**—Belief in Santa Claus is not something that has a dominant, life-forming influence on the child. He only needs to be concerned with Santa as the day of judgment (Christmas) approaches. So God is not One with whom we have to be concerned every day of our lives.*

We only need to worry about God when the Day of Judgment is approaching, when we know that soon we will die. And then we don't need to be overly concerned, as long as we can say we've done our best.

No one has ever yet got cinders and ashes in their stockings have they?

Secondly, playing the Santa Claus game can have a harmful effect upon the child's relationship to his parents. The child looks to his parents to furnish everything that he needs—food when he's hungry, love when he's lonely, comfort when he's hurt, courage when he's afraid, and truth when he asks questions. When his bright eyes look up at you and he says with all seriousness, "Can Santa's reindeer really fly" what will you say? If you answer, "Yes, Rudolph and the others really can fly," then you are no longer playing a game. You are lending your personal authority to the myth, giving it the ring of reality. He who has always trusted you for the truth, now believes you. The lie becomes truth for the child. And children will actually fight their playmates to defend the credibility of their parents. "My daddy says..." can be a fierce battle-cry in the small world of children. Time moves on, and the child begins to see that his parents have been pulling the wool over his eyes and laughing behind his back all these years. It begins to dawn on him that he made a fool out of himself fighting for what Mom and Dad said was true. What happens to their credibility now? Why should he believe what they say, let alone stick his neck out to defend them? Sadder, but wiser, he asks himself how he can ever be sure that they aren't fooling him again. That relationship that was characterized by trust and confidence is now shot full of holes; doubt and suspicion linger long in the child's mind.

Thirdly, the Santa Claus myth can have a harmful effect upon the child's faith-relationship with the true and living God. He once believed in a man with God-like qualities who turned out to be a fake. Why should he commit himself again to belief in a man who claimed to be God manifested in the flesh? If you get burned once, it's pretty silly to put your hand back on the stove, isn't it? Mom & Dad and even the television newsmen told him about Santa Claus, and it was just a trick. How can he be sure that Mom and Dad and the pastor aren't all trying to pull the wool over his eyes now? If Santa was just for little kids, maybe Jesus is just for older kids. But still just for kids. The gospel may turn out to be only another God-game, after all (Schulz: *Idols—Dead or Alive?* pp. 143-147).

Many of the traditions and traits of the ancient Saint Nicholas and the early American Sinter Klaes are still embodied in today's Santa Claus. Time may have added wrinkles, pounds, a new suit, nine flying reindeer, and an ecumenical and global flavor.

But the core remains the same. At the core are the false doctrines of idolatry which I shall enumerate in the following paragraphs.

Work Righteousness
Idolatry seeks a human solution to human problems. Man needs to atone for his evil. Whether a particular cult/-ism/philosophy employs animal sacrifices, human sacrifices, self flagellation, or an emphasis on good deeds and community service, the aim is for the followers to pay for their sins themselves. In previous chapters we have seen the exact same thing in the Saint Nicholas/Santa Claus cult. Little children are urged to "be good little boys and girls." Stories of the saint feature him admonishing mortals, whether they are sailors, thieves, innkeepers or fathers to stop their godless activity and to do something to make reparations for the wrongs which they have committed.

Scripture clearly teaches that no one can atone for his or her sins. The writer to the Hebrews instructs us: *because it is impossible for the blood of bulls and goats to take away sins* (Hebrews 10:4). Paul wrote to the church in Rome: *Therefore no one will be declared righteous in his sight by observing the law; rather, through the law we become conscious of sin* (Romans 3:20). To the Galatians Paul wrote: *Clearly no one is justified before God by the law, because, "The righteous will live by faith"* (Galatians 3:11).

There is only one who can extricate mankind from its predicament—the God-man Jesus Christ. It is his blood, shed on Calvary, which cleanses us clean from sin in the sight of God. Nothing we can do will aid in our salvation, despite what Santa says about "being good little boys and girls."

Nature of God
The myths and legends that have come to us via Saint Nicholas and Santa Claus also reflect on a false theology about the nature of God. This misperception comes in several flavors.

First, the nature of God becomes one of an angry Judge, promising good things to those who are good and curses and punishments to the evil. It denies the fact that the true Triune God has promised his blessing and salvation to all who repent and trust in Christ for forgiveness for all sin.

Other elements of the myth portray a god who is kind and grandfatherly. This comes when we realize that "Santa" really doesn't leave cinders, ashes, coal or sticks to the bullies we know (or even when we are afraid that our conduct hasn't been up to snuff for Christmas presents). The feeling sets in that God just winks at sin, he doesn't really punish. Therefore, no one sees a need to repent. (Ironically, idolatry often bypasses repentance. If the adherents can purchase their salvation, or earn it or place blame elsewhere, then why repent and turn away from sin? We can always make up for it later!).

God also is seen as distant and far off. If the benevolent Saint Nick is up there at the North Pole and sneaking peeks during December when and where we can't see him, then where is God? We can't see him, hear his voice, touch him or feel his presence. Thus God must be off far away in heaven and has no care or concern for what happens here on earth.

The fact that children put their trust in this myth which our culture has created and cultivated over the centuries is of concern. They become dependant upon this "savior" who can provide for their physical needs and wants. This character does nothing for the child's spiritual growth, but in fact retards if not destroys that growth. As parents we need to draw the line between Santa and Christ. If we allow our children to grow up believing in the reality of Santa and his benevolence, only to be devastated when the child realizes that it is all a hoax, then we need to realize that the child will also have grave reservations and doubts about Christ and the Bible. To drive our children away from the gospel message of full and free forgiveness through this myth would indeed be an action with dire consequences. We would do well to take to heart Jesus' admonition:

> And if anyone causes one of these little ones who believe in me to sin, it would be better for him to be thrown into the sea with a large millstone tied around his neck. (Mark 9:42).

Santa Claus: Is He For Your Child?

CHAPTER FOURTEEN
Are Saint Nicholas and Santa Claus the Same?
Or Are they Diametric Opposites?

Throughout this book I have equated Saint Nicholas and Santa Claus. At times I have used both proper names. At others I have interchanged the names. Obviously in tracing the history I used "Saint Nicholas" for the worldview and "Santa Claus" for the American view to reflect the terms used at each point in history. In today's culture we often use the two interchangeably. Many even have as part of their family Christmas tradition where St. Nick comes on December 6 to pick up his letters so that he knows what to deliver on December 24 (obviously Santa has some fast working elves to build all the toys in two weeks). Our secular carols, stories, tales, ads, and culture all look at Saint Nicholas and Santa Claus as one and the same.

Imagine my surprise, however, when I was reprimanded and told, in no uncertain terms, that these were two different people; one benevolent, kind and helpful to pious people while the other was merely a god of materialism. Not surprisingly my lecture came from a Sister of the Roman Church. During my studies at the seminary I worked in the kitchen of a motherhouse, or convent. On December 6 all the employees received little bags of goodies for Saint Nicholas' Day. Being ignorant I asked if this was from "Santa Claus." Thus the reason for my immediate lesson.

What is very ironic about the whole episode is that to help support the retired Sisters the more able Sisters make and sell ceramics. A major part of their sales is in the making and selling of Santa Clauses! Here there is no distinction made. You can purchase Saint Nicholases all the way from the Turkish bishop of the fourth century to the Saints of Western Europe as portrayed in the nineteenth century. Included among them, to complete your set, are the various American Santa Clauses (often based on the drawings of Thomas Nast)! Obviously what was practiced differed from what was preached.

The "materialistic" Santa was also portrayed in another, rather popular, pose at the convent. It featured Santa, in full red uniform, kneeling by the manger. Can one then really say that Santa is that evil?

The point is this, that there is no difference between the Saint and Santa. To try to differentiate between the two can only be a matter of semantics. The essence of the two characters are the same. To call Santa evil because he is a worldly, materialistic figure universally loved regardless of race, creed, or religion is to close one's eyes to the fact that Saint Nicholas throughout the ages possessed the same attributes. And as we have seen in the many colorful legends about the Saint, his beliefs, methods, and message are not very different from the Santa which we know today. As I have related these legends I have strived to point out those similarities.

Both of these figures are similar in one very critical area. They both espouse teachings and beliefs that are diametrically opposed to the message of Jesus Christ. The Gospel message is one of full and free forgiveness of all sins for all people throughout all ages through the blood of Christ alone. Saint Nicholas and Santa Claus both preach work-righteousness (you better be good, you better be nice...). Saint Nicholas, when he allegedly performed miracles or allegedly appeared to evil people, always urged people to lead good and godly lives—but never mentions what Jesus Christ has done! Much like the mythology of Rome and Greece, Saint Nick is a picture and model of goodness and virtue. By following this example one can secure a better life for himself or herself.

Santa Claus also demands that we be good (although "good" is never defined. We must all be good because we all get something good from Santa!). He promises earthly treasures and earthly blessings. Obviously, Nick and Santa are not pointing us to "things above" but to "earthly things." This focus can only undermine the Gospel message of Christ and either instill or reinforce a greater dependence upon work righteousness or a rejection of all things that are of a spiritual nature. This rejection comes both because the standards of legalism are greater than any person can fulfill and because there is disillusionment from being lied to.

Saint Nicholas and Santa Claus are inextricably linked together. Santa is no more secular or worldly than Saint Nicholas; Saint Nicholas is no more virtuous, godly, benevolent, kind or helpful than Santa. The message of both undermine the true message of Christmas and the Gospel. Both rob us of the true Christmas joy. Both stand for the same philosophy, beliefs and actions. It is of utmost importance to keep the two linked together as we know them today.

Hopefully you, the reader, have come to this conclusion by yourself in reading this book. The comparisons are there. Let no one convince you otherwise.

CHAPTER FIFTEEN
In Conclusion...

This book is the result mainly of personal experiences in my daily life as a Christian. Often people with whom I worked have asked religious questions when they discovered that I once attended a seminary. There has been a common barrier in many conversations—what theologians call the *lex opiniones*, or the opinion of the Law. We all have the Law written in our hearts. Through its voice, known as the conscience, it reminds us what is right and what is wrong. It also criticizes and condemns when we have failed. Conscience may become blunt in some areas and sharper in others. But it has one constant. It will always tell us that we must please God or try to.

This opinion of the Law is, as Luther says, a daily companion. The Gospel is seldom a guest in our lives. The Gospel only comes to us through the means of Grace—God's inspired and inerrant word and his Sacraments of Baptism and Holy Communion.

In these means of Grace we find full and free forgiveness. Here we receive that message that God himself has paid the full price for all of our sins on the cross. We are redeemed. We are now God's own children.

What does this have to do with this treatise on Santa Claus? When someone sees the story of Santa Claus as a myth which their parents, and sometimes their Church, has fed them during their childhood, then the stories of Scripture will be viewed with the same skepticism. This is not a thought that I have developed off the top of my head. This is based on personal experience. All too often I have heard someone discount what Scripture says because they remember that Santa Claus was only a childhood story. And since the Santa myths have some common themes as the miracles in the Old Testament or Jesus' miracles, then it is easy to acquire a mindset that refuses to accept much of what Scripture says.

In discounting what Scripture says, one must also be forced to discount what Scripture says about salvation. Scripture says, *"the just are saved by faith"* (Habbakuk 2:4; Romans 1:17; Galatians 3:11). This was Luther's theme when he realized that his good works could not effect his salvation. Did Luther just twist and use this passage to accommodate his failings? No, he struggled with that very passage for some time, believing that he had to replicate God's righteousness, not cling to God's righteousness.

It is through faith in the righteousness that God owns and bestows upon us through the blood of Jesus Christ that alone saves us. We have no part in this path of salvation; God paid the price, God caused the Word to reach our ears and eyes and taste (Communion) and touch (Baptism) and God created the faith in our hearts by using these means of Grace.

The message of Santa, outside of creating a blockade of skepticism about Scripture, also builds and reinforces the doctrine of Good Works. We are all well aware that part of the myth of Santa Claus is that little boys and girls better be good if they want something from the kind elf/saint. Santa's first words to his young visitors are "Have you been good this year?" Of course "good" is a relative term. "Good" as opposed to what "bad" or "evil" person, place, or thing? It is never defined and, since we never know of anyone getting skipped by Santa, it is never established. We are all good since we have all received gifts. Is it not interesting that Humanism and the New Age movement also see each and every person as good? It brings to mind the responsive prayer that was found in a Unitarian/Universalist "Church" bulletin that states that we will all be found in heaven together with Luther, St. Francis of Assisi, Hitler, Stalin, VCRs and our personal computers. I have no doubt that Hitler and Stalin themselves received gifts from Saint Nicholas, but I doubt whether we will see them in heaven.

The true message of Christmas can only be found in the manger and at the cross.

Why did God become man and dwell among us? Why did this one man, innocent of any crimes against the state, have to die on the cross? I doubt that if the Bible was merely a book to highlight the injustice against individuals, as the crucifixion of Christ would be a foremost example, then it wouldn't contain passages such as Romans 13:1-7. Scripture's message is of Sin and Grace, Law and Gospel. It tells us that we are sinful from birth, that we daily commit sins against God and that we can never repay the debt for our sins nor can we hope to be perfect. Scripture also gives us the Good News that by faith alone we are saved through the perfect life and innocent death of Jesus Christ. Salvation is our possession. Salvation is our life through Christ. In order to pay the price God demanded Jesus had to be *born of a woman, born under law, to redeem those under law, that we might receive the full rights of sons* (Galatians 4:4,5). Only by living a perfect life could Jesus die an innocent death, which is the payment God decreed for the forgiveness of all sins. Just as sin entered by one man, so also salvation comes by one man. As parents we need to be concerned about the message of Santa over against the message of Christ. Do we really want to risk our children's eternal future on the myths and humorous stories of a saint-turned-elf? No doubt we need to address to our children who that jolly, red-suited elf is when we see him all over television and in the malls. But let's be honest. It is a hoax. We know that what Santa is and what he stands for isn't true. What is true and what does have substance is the reason why we even celebrate Christmas. Without the baby in the manger, Christmas would probably still be the Saturnalia festival of ancient Rome or some other godless celebration. Christmas is more than gifts and being good and having goodwill towards each other for a few select weeks.

It is about God's gift and our righteousness given to us by God through the blood of his Son and the peace and goodwill that Christ's sacrifice has brought between God and mankind.

Hopefully this book will help each of us as parents and Christians to know the truth behind Santa Claus and Saint Nicholas. Hopefully we can concentrate on the ultimate message of Christmas. By God's grace we are now his children. Let us not allow some pagan myth with a distorted message to take this treasure away. Satan has enough tools at his disposal. Let us not give him another in the form of Santa Claus.

BIBLIOGRAPHY

BOOKS

——; *Basic Catechism.* 1980: Daughters of St. Paul, Boston, MA.

——; *The Book of Christmas.* 1985: The Readers' Digest Association, Pleasantville, NY.

——; *Concordia Triglotta.* 1921: Concordia Publishing House, St. Louis, MO.

——; *A Family Christmas.* 1984: The Readers' Digest Association, Pleasantville, NY.

——; *"Yes, Virginia".* 1972: Elizabeth Press, New York.

Conway, Msgr. John Donald; *Facts of the Faith.* 1961: All Saints Press, New York.

Crichton, Robin; *Who is Santa Claus? The True Story Behind a Living Legend.* 1987: The Bath Press, Bath, England.

Durant, Will; *The Story of Civilization: The Age of Faith (Volume 4).* 1950: Simon and Schuster, New York.

Ebon, Martin; *Saint Nicholas: Life and Legend.* 1975: Harper and Row, New York.

Farrell, Walter and Healy, Martin; *My Way of Life: Pocket Edition of Saint Thomas—The Summa Simplified for Everyone.* 1952: Confraternity of the Precious Blood, Brooklyn, NY.

Giblin, James Cross; *The Truth About Santa Claus.* 1985: Thomas Y. Crowell, New York.

Hamilton, Edith; *Mythology: Timeless Tales of Gods and Heroes.* 1940: New American Library of World Literature, Inc., New York.

Irving, Washington; *Diedrich Knickerbocker's A History of New York From the Beginning of the World to the End of the Dutch Dynasty.* 1880: G. P. Putnam's Sons, New York.

Jones, E. Willis; *The Santa Claus Book.* 1976: Walker and Company, New York.

Luther, Martin (Pelikan, Jaroslav, ed.); *Luther's Works.* 1955: Concordia Publishing House, St. Louis, MO.
    Vol. 2: Lectures on Genesis Chapters 6-14
    Vol. 14: Selected Psalms III
    Vol. 23: Sermons on the Gospel of Saint John, Chapters 6-8
    Vol. 39: Church and Ministry I
    Vol. 45: The Christian in Society

M'Clintock, Rev. John, D.D. and Strong, James, S.T.D.; *Cyclopaedia of Biblical, Theological, and Ecclesiastical Literature.* 1877: Harper and Brothers, Publishers, New York.

Metford, J. C. J.; *Dictionary of Christian Lore and Legend.* 1983: Thames and Hudson, Ltd., London.

Ripley, Rev. Francis J.; *This is the Faith.* 1960: Guild Press, Publishers, New York.

Schulz, Reuel J.; *Idols—Dead or Alive?;* 1982: Northwestern Publishing House, Milwaukee, WI.

Shakespeare, William; *The Complete Works of William Shakespeare.* 1975: Avenel Books, New York.

Snyder, Phillip; December 25th.: *The Joys of Christmas Past.* 1985: Dodd, Mead and Company, New York.

Stapleton, Michael; *The Illustrated Dictionary of Greek and Roman Mythology.* 1978: Peter Bedrick Books, New York.